"What Do I Do With My Hands?"

A Guide to Acting for the Singer

Rhonda Carlson

What her students are saying...

"Rhonda gets you 'there' quicker than any teacher I've ever encountered. Now, not only do I have a book that works for me, but I have a book that will be a constant companion for my own teaching."
Chrissie Carpenter Oppedisano, Voice Teacher/Performer, Rome, Italy

"Rhonda teaches you to accept challenges while pushing your boundaries. As a pop artist, she taught me to tell a story and not just sing, giving me something that sets me apart from my peers."
Court Alexander, Lead Singer, "Mirror Talk"/Recording Artist

"This is the teacher you carry with you the rest of your life. Her approach to teaching leaves you thinking about the lesson long after the class, and her insight and gentle, but relentless, persistence produces more breakthrough performances than any teacher I know."
Benjamin Row, Featured actor, "Ragged Isle"/Irene Ryan Nominee

"This was the first teacher to clearly articulate the concept of acting and singing to me. She teaches the concepts that make you versatile and prepares you for the real world of theatre. Through her teaching, I learned that failures are to be embraced and that obstacles are fuel for the fire every actor needs to succeed."
Ned Donovan, Music Theatre Graduate, Ithaca College

"From voice to movement to style, Rhonda's instruction is highly beneficial. Her technique for character exploration has helped me consistently deliver strong performances. Without it, I wouldn't have been one of twelve performers accepted out of several hundred at Emerson."
Molly Pietroski, Theatre Major, Emerson College

"I know that I was the second student of Rhonda's in two years to achieve early acceptance at NYU TISCH. Rhonda taught me how to be versatile and theatrically believable by connecting all the elements of music theatre performance together. I knew why I was doing what I was doing, and that has made all the difference."
Chrissy Albanese, Senior-TISCH School of the Arts-NYU

Musical Theatre/Acting/Singing/Performing Arts

What Do I Do With My Hands?
A Guide to Acting for the Singer

© 2015 Second Edition
© 2013

Rhonda Carlson
Las Vegas, NV USA
email: rhondacarlsonstudio@yahoo.com

www.RhondaCarlsonStudio.com

Cover Design by: Elle Phillips
Cover photography by: Tim Harbour

Personal Dynamics Publishing
www.PersonalDynamicsPublishing.com

ISBN: 978-0-9890889-2-3

Dedication

To my husband, Kevan, who understands this material better than anyone I know. His knowledge, creative ideas, love and encouragement made this book possible.

And to my daughters, Laura and Kayla; my parents, Ted and Laura; and my brothers, Todd and Troy. Your love and support mean everything to me.

TABLE OF CONTENTS

PART II

The Wine and the Bottle
Feeling and Form

PREFACE

"What do I do with my hands?" This is the most common question I'm asked in my acting workshops for singers. The participants are looking to me for a quick fix to an uncomfortable situation, but if I were to give them arbitrary gestures without any sense of purpose, I would be teaching empty mimicry, not art. Unlike a static painting or sculpture, singing and acting are both art forms that move through time and, when combined, they require a unique set of tools. If I can provide these tools and guide students through a process that marries these two art forms in a symbiotic, holistic way, the students will learn to be artists as they explore, discover, reveal, react, and express.

Although this book primarily deals with the principles of acting, it is an acting approach that is specifically designed for the singer. It is not a substitute for acting classes, private instruction, and the performance experience, but it will hopefully provide the connective fiber that many singers are missing.

Once performers learn that failure is a natural road to success, they will begin to actually enjoy the rewarding process of making artistic choices. Once they embrace a philosophy, clearly understand artistic concepts, and have a willingness to be risk-takers, they will learn that tools and techniques are not an end, but a means to something greater. And once they figure this out, they will know exactly what to do with their hands.

Rhonda Carlson

ACKNOWLEDGEMENTS

Special thanks to...

Ken Owens, my publisher, for his wisdom and inspiring advice.

Tim Harbour, photographer, and Elle Phillips, cover designer, for their creative vision and technical artistry.

Maggie Mascari for her sense of fun, as evidenced in her delightful image on the cover.

Camille Duskin, and Ken and Jenny Kucan for their unwavering support of the arts and the artist.

My husband, Kevan, for his artistic advice, technical support, and management sensibilities.

My daughter, Laura, for her literary wisdom and technical wizardry.

My daughter, Kayla, for inspiring my visual imagination.

My parents, Ted and Laura, for their unconditional love and unwavering support for all of my endeavors.

The performing arts teachers who changed my life: Lyle Meredith, Bill Lilley, Bill Wilson, Juanita Moran, Henri Robbins, Erma Johnson, Norman Gulbrandsen, David Vornholt, and Wilma English.

My students, who continually challenge and inspire me to be a better teacher.

FOREWORD
by
John Freedson
Producer - Forbidden Broadway

When Rhonda asked me to write the foreword for her book, I laughed and thought, "Why me? When I was an actor, I never knew what to do with my hands. That's why I became a producer!" Then it occurred to me: because I have spent a good portion of my career working in the genres of parody and comedy, I'm an excellent person to ask! The performers we cast in *Forbidden Broadway*, those who are able to truly succeed at what we ask them to do in our musical comedy / parody / impersonation niche, have to be terrific actors! Why? Because comedy is one of the most difficult genres to do well. Add the musical element to that and there are even fewer who succeed. As all successful musical theatre comedians have learned, "It's all about connecting!" You have to be able to connect to the character, connect to the music, connect to the movement, and connect to the material. Then, you must learn how to combine all of those into one cohesive, truthful, and entertaining performance. And you have to do all of that within the confines of a non-flexible musical score.

Which leads me to Rhonda's book. Sure, some people can do it all because they know it instinctively. But, more often than not, everyone has got to find a "way", a "technique," they can depend on to find and maintain all of these connections, especially the most important connection of all—the connection between the performer and the audience. Rhonda understands this, and she knows how to teach this "connection" business. And she does it in a positive and insightful way that explains "why" as well as "how."

The great Carol Channing once said, "Laughter is much more important than applause. Applause is almost a duty. Laughter is a reward." That connection, that indescribable reward we get when we connect to an audience, whether it's to make them laugh or cry, is the magic in what we do.

At *Forbidden Broadway*, we have had the unique opportunity to parody some of the greatest performers in all of musical theater, many of them our idols. Although they come from all strata of society and points of origin, if I had to say what they all have in common, it would be an extraordinary ability for risk-taking. I'm not talking about jumping out of a plane. I'm talking about the people who have learned that making a bad choice is not synonymous with failing.

The arts have always been about taking risks, and Rhonda's book is a guide to risk-taking. It challenges the reader to look inside, muster the strength to put fear aside, and make the connections necessary to create a fully-realized performance. So many people perform, so few affect an audience. So many teachers teach, so few actually affect their students. Rhonda not only affects her students, she will affect anyone who is lucky enough to read this book.

John Freedson

"There is a vitality, a life force, an energy, a quickening that is translated through you into action, and because there is only one of you in all of time, this expression is unique. And if you block it, it will never exist through any other medium and it will be lost. The world will not have it. It is not your business to determine how good it is nor how valuable nor how it compares with other expressions. It is your business to keep it yours clearly and directly, to keep the channel open. You do not even have to believe in yourself or your work. You have to keep yourself open and aware to the urges that motivate you. Keep the channel open. No artist is pleased. [There is] no satisfaction whatever at any time. There is only a queer divine dissatisfaction, a blessed unrest that keeps us marching and makes us more alive than the others."

Martha Graham

What Do I Do With My Hands?

A Guide to Acting for the Singer

INTRODUCTION

You've worked hard on breath support and posture. You've successfully navigated your vocal bridges and have a solid high C. You've learned the notes, mastered the rhythms, and memorized the lyrics. Although you're still confused about what to do with your hands, you have a short list of "moves" that are dependable—upward palms, a gentle shake of the head for emphasis, an occasional soulful grimace with furrowed eyebrows, and, for the up-tempo endings, a pair of snazzy jazz hands. You've arrived! On the other hand, your most enthusiastic applause comes from family members, directors are happy to have you in the chorus but never call you back for the lead, and your best singing engagements are at karaoke bars on Saturday nights. Obviously, something is missing.

The good news? You have a vocal technique that gives you a dependable and flexible musical foundation. The bad news? Basically, you've learned to shoot the basket and dribble the ball, but you haven't played the game. Your vocal technique has become an end, rather than a means to something greater. Without the tools to effectively convey the meaning of the song, you might as well perform vocal exercises for your audience. However, if you can master tools and techniques that give you a more complete performance, your excellent vocal technique will serve your artistry.

For the painter, the brush is the instrument for expression and the paint that is applied to that brush is the medium. For the singing actor, your voice and body are the "brush", and your life experiences and the life experiences of those you've observed are the "paint" on that brush. Even the most advanced computer can't duplicate the emotional expression of a human being. This emotional life you experience and share is intuitive and complex, and occurs moment-by-moment. When you respond to a thought or an action, your entire being kicks in; your breath, your voice, your gestures, your posture, and your eyes all work together in a natural way. This is why one broad, arbitrary gesture "indicating" you are sad or happy simply doesn't ring true to your audience, and it certainly doesn't give you anywhere to go artistically. You could try and take an inventory to implement a full body of responses, but because you live in a world of fast-paced, instant-to-instant reactions, there would be no way to keep up with these physical cues in a convincing way.

> *"Acting is the ability to live truthfully under given imaginary circumstances."* **Sanford Meisner**

The best way to understand acting is to take a look at how we emotionally respond in real life. For example, if, as an actor, you are playing someone who has just learned he or she has won the lottery, your first choice might be to jump up and down and scream, "I won! I won!" However, the *actual* response in this situation is more complex. If you could break down the real reactions and observe them in slow motion, beat by beat, you might discover more.

Your initial internal reaction might be:

"You mean me?"

Followed by:

"But wait, did I play my usual numbers this week?"

Then, you glance at your friend who has delivered the news.

"Oh my gosh, we bought the ticket together at the quick shop two days ago. Didn't we?"

Your friend's wide grin answers your question.

"Yes, it's true. It must be me."

And a split second later, you jump up and down and scream:

"I won! I won!"

This all takes place in a fraction of a second, so the details simply can't be achieved with a checklist. On the other hand, if you opt for a generic "happy and excited" response, something will be missing for you and your audience. Instead, you must learn the acting tools for a process that will open your eyes and get you in touch with the feelings and reactions that lead to effective theatrical and musical expression. It is a process that takes you and your audience along for an empathetic, intuitive, and emotionally connected ride.

> *"We do not remember days; we remember moments."*
> *Cesare Pavese*

TOOLS FOR THE ACTING SINGER

Just as there are tools for singing, painting, dancing, and writing, there are tools for acting. By using IMAGERY (your imagination) and SENSE MEMORY (remembering how something looked, sounded, tasted, felt, or smelled), you can throw away your list of planned gestures and fixed gazes, and instead, access honest and effective emotional responses. It's not enough, however, to merely "feel" something on stage. Acting is a "to do" endeavor that must be shared. Consequently, you must learn how to express and integrate these emotions into a work of art. Since acting and singing are art forms that move through time, you must learn tools for a process that moves through time. Once you can depend on these tools, you will be able to make strong choices rather than being at the mercy of wishful thinking and phony gestures. You will have developed an acting technique that is as dependable as your singing technique.

THE SINGING ACTOR

As a singing actor, you will require a more disciplined and concrete acting technique than that of a non-singing actor. This is because you are more confined by the elements of time and musical accompaniment. Your acting moments may be dictated by quarter-note rests, presto tempos, soaring modulations, or eight-bar interludes. You can't wait for inspiration when you must make a theatrical choice in eight counts. Even your mood and emotional state may be influenced by a dark modal key or a frenetic sequence of chromatic runs. This confinement, however, can produce a powerful and moving performance if you learn how to use it to your advantage.

> *"You must have chaos within you to give birth to a dancing star."*   *Friederick Nietziche*

THE LEARNING PROCESS AND YOUR BRAIN

Before you begin, it's important to understand that learning to act isn't a simple step-by-step, how-to list of instructions. Certainly, there are specific tools and outlined processes that can be broken down into bite-sized servings, but there's more to it than simply finding the right answers to your questions. Instead, it's about learning a process that inspires you to make the *strongest choices*.

Your individual choices are the foundation to your creativity. Think about it. "Choice" is what makes you...you. What you wear, who you hang out with, what you eat, and where you live are all choices that affect your life on a daily basis.

Whether you are making life choices or artistic ones, you must use both sides of your brain. Your intellectual choices, primarily a function of your left-brain, are less messy than your emotional ones. This informational left side of your brain can analyze life with a list of "do's and don'ts" and corresponding consequences. This is the side of your brain that handles the logistics of memorization, staging, and musical accuracy.

Your right brain is where your emotional and creative choices are made. This part of your brain is less concrete and more intuitive than your left brain. Since, as an artist, you are after the best choice rather than the right answer, you will be required to give in to a trial-and-error process while exploring this side of your brain. This process will lead you to a path for artistic expression. One discovery will lead to another, and you will have an endless flow of ideas and experiences that will continually challenge you to make strong and effective choices.

> *"Creativity is allowing yourself to make mistakes. Art is knowing which ones to keep."*   **Scott Adams**

FAILURE

"Failure" is not a dirty word. When it comes to creativity, failure is required! In fact, it must be embraced. Acting is not only a process; it is a process of elimination. When you fail, you've simply eliminated a weak choice to make way for a stronger one.

Failure can actually be rewarding because it will bring you closer and closer to a desired outcome. It's a little like shopping for the perfect outfit or a brand new car. It's messy and frustrating sometimes, but it can actually be a lot of fun. And when a process is enjoyable, you will be less inhibited and more open to new ideas. Again, you are seeking the *strongest choice*, not the *right answer*. Therefore, you must explore the limitless possibilities by taking big risks. After all, how do you know where the edge is if you haven't gone over it?

> *"We all know that ART is not truth. Art is a lie that makes us realize truth, at least the truth that is given us to understand. The artist must know the manner whereby to convince others of the truthfulness of his lies."*
> **Pablo Picasso**

TRUTH

Granted, few people break out into song after drinking a poisonous potion or reuniting with a long-lost lover, but when music and drama coincide, you and your audience will be transported to a new level of experience. This musical and theatrical expression that would be absurd in real life is emotionally transforming in performance, and when it is done right, it creates a powerful aesthetic connection that reveals profound truths that simply can't be explained in mere words.

> *"The greatest feat of human beings is that we have the power of empathy, we can all sense a mysterious connection to each other."*   *Meryl Streep*

People want to be moved, and there's something about the safety of a dark theatre that gives them permission to feel something they might not be comfortable with in the real world. The theatre is where they can feel empathy, wonder, hope, love, and inspiration, and, sometimes, that's all in one night.

This ineffable connection the arts have with human feeling is magical. Someone sitting in the last row of the balcony, someone you have never met, will wipe away a tear, will laugh in spite of a forlorn heart, or will rage at an injustice. And who knows? You, as the artist, might even change your own heart as you explore and express the human condition. You might even indirectly help change the world. Maybe this is why artists are often the visionaries in a society, ridiculed as strange while living, and later worshipped as genius when the masses finally understand their vision.

> *"I really think that effective acting has to do literally with the movement of molecules."*   *Glenn Close*

PART I

The Hills are Alive...in the Fourth Wall

Imagery and Sense Memory

Chapter 1

THE WHOM

"Who is that spot on the wall?"

"I regard the theatre as the greatest of all art forms, the most immediate way in which a human being can share with another the sense of what it is to be a human being."
Oscar Wilde

You are a storyteller. We all are in one way or another. Some people can get up in front of a large crowd and make the most mundane story into a sidesplitting comedy act, but most of us share our stories in a routine way to family, friends, and colleagues. How you tell a story has a lot to do with WHOM you are speaking to. For example, you are probably more animated and natural when you speak to people you are close to and more reserved and formal when you speak to a bank clerk or potential employer.

THE WHOM

If you are performing in a play or musical, for the most part, you'll be speaking and singing to the cast members on stage with you. Some of your most moving moments, however, will be when you are singing or speaking alone on stage. Singers, in particular, frequently perform musical monologues that are usually delivered into the fourth wall—the area where the audience resides. Unless you are delivering your material directly to the audience, you will need to convey the song to someone in your imagination. This is your WHOM image. Unfortunately, most singers forget about the WHOM and sing to no one in particular while occasionally throwing in some random gestures. This "pick a spot on the wall" gaze and these meaningless gestures distract from your performance. If you told a story in real life this way, people would think you were dishonest and disengaged, the last thing you want to be as a performer.

> *"The word 'theatre' comes from the Greeks. It means 'seeing place.' It is the place people come to see the truth about life and the social situation."* **Stella Adler**

FIRST THINGS FIRST

The first thing you should ask yourself when you are performing a song is "To WHOM am I singing?" The delivery of your material will depend on it. Think about how singing "Happy Birthday" to a college friend at his rowdy birthday bash would differ than singing "Happy Birthday" to your three-year-old niece as she drifts off to sleep. You wouldn't think of singing it the same way, yet singers will often provide the same gaze, posture, and gestures for every single song in their repertoire.

Next, you should ask yourself WHY you are singing the song. You can sing "Mary Had a Little Lamb" to a group of friends to provide a heartfelt eulogy for the lamb. On the other hand, you can sing the same song to the same friends, desperately trying to convince them that Mary isn't crazy. There really *is* a lamb that is trying to follow her to school. It's the same WHOM, the same text, but there is a different reason for singing it.

IMAGERY

Words and images are natural partners, and throughout the course of this book, you will learn how to access IMAGERY (seeing something in your imagination), and SENSE MEMORY (recalling how something looked, sounded, smelled, tasted, and/or felt). If you don't use SENSE MEMORY, you may have trouble connecting to your emotions. If you don't use IMAGERY, you may have trouble connecting with your eyes and your gestures. It would be a little like showing off the gold in the fabric of your new sofa to a friend without ever looking at the sofa or your friend. Yet, singers will often punctuate their songs with gestures that have no visual reference, no connection to the image or the related emotion.

> **Note: Sometimes, when singers are asked, "Who are you singing to?" they will reply, "myself." This is rarely a strong choice because it doesn't allow them to project their energy into the fourth wall. The result? Closed eyes and a "lost in my own world" approach that doesn't connect with the audience. Even though you will have inner moments in a song, it can be helpful to sing or speak to a trusted confidant or an imaginary childhood friend, even if you are technically "singing to yourself".**

CREATING YOUR CHARACTER'S RELATIONSHIP

Although this fourth wall WHOM image may be "made up", it's helpful to draw on memories of actual people you've known in your life in order to connect to and elaborate on the image you're singing to. As you've learned, it's not enough to simply make up a WHOM; you must also decide on WHY you're singing. In order to decide on WHY, you must determine your relationship with the WHOM. And, in order to determine your relationship, you must know who *you* are as the character. At first this may seem a little daunting until you realize that you are already a variety of characters with a variety of relationships in your everyday life. You are one person when you're with your grandmother at Sunday dinner and another one with your friends at a football game. For the actor, the trick is learning to borrow from yourself *and* from others.

> *"The idea of "just being yourself" is a total abstraction, for we are many selves and we wear many masks."*
> *Robert Cohen*

THE WHY

Why are you singing or speaking to your WHOM in the first place? What are the circumstances? Are you anxious to share gossip with your best friend? Are you afraid to tell your mom you wrecked her car? Are you begging your lover to stay with you? Your relationship with the image is going to directly affect the emotional delivery of your material. If your WHOM and your relationship with the WHOM are specific, your performance will be more connected, more believable. Specific responses simply evoke more emotion than general ones. For example, singing to your mother who is lovingly and hastily sewing a button on your tux coat just before your first prom will move you more than a "generic son" singing to a "generic mother." Singing to your dad when he has told you you're beautiful in spite of your braces and freckles is going to evoke more emotion from you than simply singing to "a dad."

ACTIVE IMAGES

If your WHOM is going to be specific and real, he or she must be more than a stationary spot on the wall. Instead, your WHOM must be living, breathing, and responding in your mind's eye. As you respond to your WHOM, your WHOM should respond to you, which, in turn, will affect your next response, and so on—sort of like playing catch with a ball. If your WHOM turns away from you, you may naturally reach out. If your WHOM gets in your face, you may retreat. This give-and-take will create a full circle of reactions, and, when this happens, you will be communicating with an ACTIVE IMAGE instead of a cardboard cut-out, stationary image, illustrating one of the most important rules for the actor: "Acting is reacting."

> NOTE: Sometimes you will "watch" your WHOM in the fourth wall rather than directly sing or speak to him or her. You may sing *about* your lover's flaxen hair as she dances in the wind, or you may watch your young son digging in the sand as you sing a song about how good life has been. Even though you are not speaking directly to this WHOM, the image should still be active in order for it to affect your delivery.

KEEP THE AUDIENCE OUT OF IT

For the most part, you will respond to your WHOM in the fourth wall so that the audience can see your full face. (It's very difficult to read human emotion when looking at a profile.) Unless you are speaking or singing directly to the audience members as a narrator or a performer in a live band, don't look directly at them. They are not part of your fantasy if you are performing a role. Instead, keep the imagery just above their heads so they can watch you respond to your image without feeling like *they* are the image. This is especially true in auditions, even though your "audience" may only be a few feet away.

WHEN YOUR AUDIENCE *IS* THE WHOM IMAGE

If you are singing directly to the audience members, don't think of them as a vague mass of humanity. You will connect with them more effectively if you sing to them as an audience of individuals--the teenager in the back screaming your name or the groupie singing along in the front row. Even if you can't actually see these people because of the lights, your delivery will be more engaging if you imagine the audience this way.

IS YOUR IMAGE MADE UP OR REAL?

Studies have shown that our memories are anything but perfect. Very few of us recall actual events accurately, and, more often than not, we "remember" details that simply aren't true. We don't always do it intentionally, but when it comes to being entirely objective, we are only human. ("Ah Yes, I Remember it Well" from *Gigi* comes to mind.)

As actors, we often change the "memory" intentionally, making up new or added details for the image. We've all embellished stories from time to time or slightly changed the facts to suit our own needs. How many times does the parent get the whole story? How honest are you when someone asks, "How do I look?" Therefore, as you explore actual people, don't be afraid to use reality as a jumping off place for more imaginative details. By using your imagination, you can fill in details you may not be able to remember. What color was your date's prom dress? Don't remember? Okay, then choose "blue" to provide more sensory detail. Although your actual memories are your most vivid ones, it might be fun to give your prom date a mental makeover or change the 1996 Ford you drove in high school to a brand new Corvette, as long as you remain true to the style and intent of the material you're performing.

You can look for clues in the libretto to help embellish your WHOM and bring him or her to life. A song lyric may refer to her "red, rosy lips," or the text of a monologue may specify his "ugly, polka dot tie." Period musicals and operas, in particular, may require you to imagine beyond the scope of your experience by borrowing ideas from characters or situations you've seen on television, in movies, or in books. You may never have seen a pirate, but you can put one together in your mind by watching or reading *Peter Pan, The Pirates of the Caribbean,* or *Treasure Island.*

EXERCISES

1. *Describe someone you know out loud. Not only describe physical characteristics, but psychological and emotional ones as well. Consider voice color, energy, temperament, mannerisms, outlook on life, anything you can think of. By speaking out loud and hearing your own words, you will reinforce the emotional connections in the description. For example, you can actually respond to the tone of your own voice when you say things like "raging lunatic" or "sweet, little angel."*

2. *Once you've heard your own words, try and visualize this person in a specific place, at a specific moment. What was this person actually doing while being a "raging lunatic" (a fender bender perhaps?), or what place and circumstance*

come to mind when describing the "sweet, little angel" (your child falling asleep to a lullaby)? Ultimately, your reaction to these memories and the accompanying details will be projected into the fourth wall via your imagination. (Just like all those imaginary friends you played with when you were a kid.)

3. If you're having trouble imagining a WHOM, ask a friend to fill in for the WHOM image. While the friend is there in front of you in real time, observe him or her in action. Maybe you are watching your friend do the dishes or talk to a cashier. Then, engage your friend in conversation and notice his or her reactions. Is your friend listening sympathetically or standing in judgment? Is your friend hanging on your every word or thinking about something or someone else while you speak? How does his or her reaction affect your side of the conversation?

4. Once you've experienced a "real image", make one up. You might even add some fun details. Maybe it's your Prince Charming or an evil twin. Maybe it's your ideal boss or your idea of a thoroughly entertaining friend. When you've filled in the details of WHOM and WHY, have a conversation with the WHOM, speaking your portion of the conversation out loud while your WHOM's comments are simply made up in your head. Keep the WHOM moving and responding.

5. You may use an actual person as reference for your WHOM, but the script or song may require something more. Decide on a WHOM you know, but then expand on reality by asking yourself a series of "what if" questions. What if my shy, mild-mannered teacher suddenly lost her cool and became a terrorist? What if my grumpy old Uncle Marty was actually the tooth fairy? What if my tough friend, Jack, uncharacteristically dissolved into tears?

6. *Remember, it's not enough to describe your WHOM. It's also vital to understand your <u>relationship</u> with the WHOM since this will affect your delivery. Select a brand new WHOM. After you describe your relationship, ask yourself what the WHOM might say about <u>you</u>. Then, compare your answers. You may like your boss, but maybe he's only nice to you because your dad is the CEO of the company. An acquaintance may view you as a best friend, while you don't feel like you really know her at all. Do you both feel like you have been the bad guy, or is that merely the perception of your WHOM? How does the relationship make you feel, or, more importantly, how does it make you react? Confident? Insecure? Intimidated?*

7. *Remember and/or make up your personal history with a WHOM. How did you meet? How has your relationship changed since then? Gather all the information up to the present. Why are you now singing or speaking to this person in this particular moment? How has everything that occurred before affected the here and now? Write down and/or verbalize all of the possibilities.*

8. *Challenge yourself to add more details that go beyond a simple list of characteristics. By supplying the circumstances with the description, you learn far more about your WHOM.*

For example:

Vague: *He's fun to hang out with.*

Specific: *Fun? Are you kidding? We had a blast last Saturday. He got up and sang karaoke to old Beach Boy's tunes and added his own choreography. He was so off key, they almost threw us out.*

or

Vague: *She likes to talk on the phone.*

Specific: *I dread her phone calls. All she does is complain about work. I wish she'd just quit and get it over with.*

9. *Watch characters in movies that deal with invisible people, such as <u>Harvey</u> (with Jimmy Stewart), <u>Fantastic Four, Ghost, A League of Extraordinary Gentlemen,</u> and <u>The Hollow Man</u>. Watch how the actors react to these invisible characters. Also, keep in mind that newer movies that use CGI require actors to use their imaginations as they relate to characters that are not added until after the scenes have been filmed. Watch the actors in these imaginative films react to their invisible CGI scene partners. What reactions by the actors make the imagined characters seem real?*

10. *Select a song. Without worrying about the original character or dramatic context, decide on a WHOM. Then, decide why you are singing this song to this particular person. If the song is from a musical, change the actual character and relationship in order to stretch your imagination. For example, "Far From the Home I Love" from <u>Fiddler on the Roof</u> could be sung to your parents to explain why you're going out of state for college. Are your parents convinced? Are they angry? Are they sad? Take a pop or country song and determine a WHOM and a WHY. Are you trying to keep a particular someone from leaving you? Does your lover walk away in anger as you pour your heart out? Are you merely sharing a funny story with a good friend who is grinning from ear to ear?*

11. *Create a short monologue with an active WHOM image. Make sure you physically respond to your image's actions.*

For example:

(Your best friend angrily walks away from you after an argument.)

"Wait. I'm sorry. Come back."

(Your friend abruptly turns around and produces an obscene gesture.)

"You jerk! That's uncalled for."

(As you watch your friend stomp offstage right, you hear your mom calling for you from upstage left. She sounds distressed so you go to her.)

12. *Create a made-up character from scratch that might live in a fantasy world. You can still use references from real life. (After all, everyone has a relative who could be from another planet. Right?) Describe the WHOM and your relationship with the WHOM using all of your senses. Did you find the WHOM on another planet, a forest, or in the ocean? Could your WHOM have been a new character in* The Wiz *or* Seussical? *Finally, sing a song, any song to your WHOM that reflects your relationship and the circumstances. Have fun, but react honestly.*

THE REPERTOIRE LISTS

Although the suggested repertoire throughout this book should eventually be studied and presented comprehensively, this chapter and a number of the following chapters include repertoire that will allow you to concentrate on a specific area of study.

THE WHOM - Practice Repertoire

(*Repertoire particularly suited for ACTIVE IMAGES)

Always	Irving Berlin
Be On Your Own*	*(Nine)* M. Yeston
Buddy's Blues*	*(Follies)* S. Sondheim
Can You Find it in Your Heart	*(Footloose)* T. Snow/ D. Pitchford
Can't Take My Eyes Off of You	*(Jersey Boys)* F. Valli
Consider Yourself*	*(Oliver)* L. Bart
Getting to Know You	(*The King and I*) R. Rodgers/O. Hammerstein
Grand Knowing You	*(She Loves Me)* J. Bock/ S. Harnick
I Need You	D. Lee and T. Lane
Just the Way You Are	Billy Joel
Just You Wait, Henry Higgins*	*(My Fair Lady)* A. J. Lerner/ F. Loewe

Let's Call the Whole Thing Off*	*(Shall We Dance)* G. Gershwin/ I. Gershwin
My New Philosophy*	*(You're a Good Man, Charlie Brown)* C. Gesner
Papa's Gonna Make it Alright	*(Shenandoah)* G. Geld/ P. Udell
People Will Say We're in Love	*(Oklahoma)* R. Rodgers/ O. Hammerstein
Poor Wandering One	*(The Pirates of Penzance)* W.S Gilbert/ A. Sullivan
Oh, Is There Not One Maiden Breast*	*(The Pirates of Penzance)* W.S. Gilbert/ A. Sullivan
Show Me*	*(My Fair Lady)* A.J. Lerner/ F. Loewe
Take Me or Leave Me*	*(Rent)* J. Larson
When I First Saw You	*(Dreamgirls)* H. Krieger/ T. Eyen
Why Can't You Behave?	*(Kiss Me Kate)* C. Porter
Ya Got Trouble*	*(The Music Man)* M. Willson
You're Nothing Without Me*	*(City of Angels)* C. Coleman/ D. Zippel
You've Got Possibilities*	*(It's a Bird, It's a Plane, It's Superman)* C. Strouse

Chapter 2

THE WHERE IMAGE

The Scenery in the Fourth Wall

"Art is not what you see. It's what you make others see."
Edgar Degas

If you are singing a solo or performing a monologue in a production, the scenery on stage will provide an upstage WHERE. However, the fourth wall WHERE image that lives in your imagination (and the area where the audience just happens to reside) is the most effective one for the actor. For example, in *The Sound of Music,* the best "hills alive with music" aren't the ones on the upstage backdrop; it's the mountains Maria responds to in the fourth wall that inspire her to sing, and, in turn, move her audience as they see what she sees. The next time you're telling a story to a group of friends, stop suddenly to look at the door behind them as if you're seeing something disconcerting. More than likely, they will look behind them, expecting the worst. They will have connected to *your* WHERE image.

THE EYES CREATE THE SPACE

Remarkably, you can create a space with your physical responses without spending a dime on lumber and muslin. Your WHERE images can appear large or small, close or far away, awe-inspiring or drab, depending on the focus of your eyes, your body language, and the tone of your voice. If you're singing "I'm Flying" from *Peter Pan* in an audition, you will have to create the illusion of ascending and flying without the benefit of high wire technicians and an expensive set. When you start the song, you may respond to the WHERE directly in front of you, implying that you are at ground level in a familiar setting. As you ascend and the landscape gets smaller and broader, your focus will move downward and outward as you view and respond to the brand new world below. Your reaction may go from pleasant to awestruck as you continue the ascent. Your arms may naturally float upward, and your voice may grow louder as you call out to those below.

If you are performing "In My Own Little Corner" from Rodgers' and Hammerstein's *Cinderella,* you will initially create a cloistered WHERE in your "own little corner." You will retreat slightly with your body language and view things that are familiar and immediately within your grasp. Your body language and voice will grow, however, as the character's imagination grows—when you open your arms to embrace the applause as the "prima donna from Milan," or scan the vast landscape of the African safari. When you suddenly "hear" and "see" a lioness, you will once again retreat to the original WHERE, your "own little corner."

IMAGERY=HONEST MOVEMENT

If your WHOM and WHERE images are passive and stationary, *you* will be passive and stationary. That doesn't mean, however, that you should supply lots of unmotivated movement for your performance. The ACTIVE IMAGE simply creates an honest response, no matter how subtle or overt. You shouldn't even have to plan gestures when your imagery is active and engaged since you will probably respond in a natural way.

Note: If you can't say why you're moving, then you shouldn't move. Don't fall into the trap of "Well, I haven't moved for awhile, so I'll stroll over here and add a gesture or two." Human beings generally move when they are moving "to" or "away" from someone or something, not when they are feeling like they haven't moved enough.

HOW TO MAKE A STATIONARY WHERE IMAGE ACTIVE

If you decide to sing while you look at a stationary fourth-wall bouquet of flowers sitting on a table in your kitchen, there will be little to respond to unless you can associate these flowers with an ACTIVE IMAGE. Instead of staring at the flowers, you may find yourself smiling, even giggling, as you remember the moment you opened your office door to find your boyfriend dressed up as Cupid with the bouquet in his hand. Instead of simply staring at a sleeping child in a nursery while singing a tender ballad about him or her, you might want to remember the way the child pulled the cat's tail earlier in the day, or even imagine the child walking across the stage someday to accept a diploma.

Note: Don't just "see" the items or scenery in a WHERE—a book, a birthday cake, a hiking trail. As an actor, you must also express how you feel about the item or scenery. For example: "See that stack of bills my lazy roommate left me with." or "Your wonderful grandmother accepted my proposal on that park bench."

MUSIC AND THEATRE EXIST IN TIME!

If you are playing a country bumpkin who has just arrived in the big city (such as in the song, "Not for the Life of Me" from *Thoroughly Modern Millie)*, you shouldn't be staring at the fourth wall as if it's a picture postcard of a city skyline. Music and theatre exist in time; therefore, so should your image. Your big city WHERE should move, causing you to respond moment by moment. A group of business people may rush past you, a cab may honk and frighten you, or the sun may momentarily blind you as you search for a street sign. Simply "feeling" happy with a fixed look of wonder isn't enough to hold your interest or that of your audience, but if you fill in the details and keep your images moving, your performance will progress emotionally through time.

> *"Music is given to us with the sole purpose of establishing an order in things, including, and particularly, the coordination between man and time." Igor Stravinsky*

WHEN

The WHEN will affect your WHERE image--the season, the year, the time of day. The sunny light of a spring morning has a different look and feel than a gloomy, frigid winter evening. The cars and fashion, even the social attitudes of the 1950's, are different than those of today. When you fill in the details of the WHEN, the WHERE, and the WHOM, your imagery will certainly be more than a "spot on the wall to stare at." It will be a complete picture that will activate your senses and emotions.

EXPLORING THE SENSES

Since you experience life through your senses, it stands to reason that you'll use your senses to recreate it. "Imagery" usually refers to sight, but it is an all-inclusive word that also includes the sound, touch, smell, and taste in an environment. The *look* of the sky, the *sound* of the wind, the *feel* of a warm fire, the *sound* of the whistling teapot, the *smell* of the cookies baking in the oven, and the *taste* of your chamomile tea all help create a sensory-rich WHERE. The WHERE is a great place to explore SENSE MEMORY, but remember, it's just as important to enhance the WHOM image with sensory details. If you *see* the anger as your lover's face turns red, *feel* the sting of her slap, *hear* her screaming accusations, and *smell* the alcohol on her breath, you will certainly have a more vivid WHOM image.

> *"God gave us memories that we might have roses in December."*   *J.M. Barrie*

REVVING UP SENSE MEMORY

This collective sensory recall known as SENSE MEMORY inspires the actor. Sight, smell, hearing, touch, and taste all contribute to human feeling, so it stands to reason that your *actual* memories will be more vivid than fictional ones. Thus, it's helpful if you base your "made up" people and places on the real thing. Once you are more aware of your sensory life, you will be able to draw on it and embellish it in fictional situations. These sensory details are the ingredients for your theatrical reactions and re-creations.

Note: Acting and singing should be studied as a whole. Your vocal warm ups and technical exercises are a perfect opportunity for this. Instead of separating the singing and the acting during a warm up, let your repetitive vocal patterns be an imagery exercise as well. The "ah" vowel of a sweeping arpeggio can be your response to a vast (and detailed) panorama. You can reach out for a WHOM image as you hold the fermata at the peak of a scale. You can pop a colorful balloon for each note of a staccato pattern, or you can tell secrets to your best friend during a pianissimo exercise. Just remember to remain visually connected to the image as you sing!

> *"Acting is not being emotional, but being able to fully express emotion."*   **Kate Reid**

ACTING IS "TO DO"

Acting is reacting! You can see, feel, smell, taste, and hear until the cows come home, but if you are not reacting to these senses in an active way, you are leaving your audience out of the experience. Again, your reactions must be honest and without "indication" (as if you're trying to get someone to guess your emotion or the circumstances in a game of charades). If you can remember and re-create your reaction to an offensive odor, you might even trick your audience into thinking they smell something too. It's a matter of remembering the odor *and* remembering what you did when you smelled it.

Note: As singers, we often perform songs that do not provide a specific WHOM or WHERE. This is when creativity comes in. Assigning a WHOM and a WHERE will help you connect with the song and project energy into the fourth wall. Even though a song may not have a particular setting, you can provide the sensory details in your imagery, details that will contribute to the emotional depth of the song.

PUTTING THE WHOM IN THE ENVIRONMENT

It's not only important to decide on a WHERE for your own character; you must also determine where the WHOM resides. Are you both in the same environment or are you in contrasting ones? Are you both lost in a forest with no hope of being found? Are you sitting in a foxhole in a miserable wartime environment while the wife you are singing to in your imagination (your WHOM) is tucking the children into bed in the warm and loving environment of your home. If you are in a different environment than your WHOM, you may find yourself shifting back and forth between the two environments. For example, a young soldier might be singing "I'll Be Seeing You" from a foxhole somewhere in Europe during World War II, while he imagines his wife at home in "all the old familiar places"-- in the "small café" and "the park across the way."

WHERE IMAGES DON'T REQUIRE SET CHANGES

Once you establish your WHERE, it's also important to know that your WHERE can change on a dime. (Remember Cinderella's many adventures in "My Own Little Corner.") Although you may have determined that your song takes place in a small garden, a portion of the text may recall the time you took in the breathtaking view from the top of a high trail. The "set change" can occur instantly via your imagination and so can your response to it. Your character may start in one place, but a memory or a vision of the future may change the WHERE. In *Les Miserables*, Fantine lives in squalor when she sings "I Dreamed a Dream." As she sings, she is consumed by her dismal environment, until she begins to recall "a summer by his side." As the memory becomes more vivid, her WHERE begins to change to a place where she once experienced happiness, when her days were spent in "endless wonder." Sadly, her memory is only fleeting, and she returns to her original surroundings. In the same musical, Cosette, Fantine's young daughter, resides in a seedy tavern, but she escapes her fate by making up a new WHERE, "a castle on a cloud." This is the beauty of the imagination.

EXERCISES

1. *Walk into a room and pretend to look for a set of keys. Make it as realistic as possible, drawing on your own lost-*

key experiences. We've all had them. (Don't read ahead until you've done this.)

Next, ask someone to actually hide your keys. This time walk into the room and search until you find the keys.

Compare your pretend search reactions with your real search reactions. The actual hunt for the keys probably activated your senses in a more natural way. Instead of immediately walking in and moving pillows and hastily pushing aside books, you probably briefly looked at the person who hid the keys for a tiny body-language clue. You probably took longer to survey the layout of the room before you began searching. (Remember the moment-by-moment action discussed in the Introduction.) When you actually started looking for the keys, you probably dug deeper and explored more thoroughly.

Now, have someone hide the keys again. This time play the game "Hot and Cold" as you look for the keys. Notice how engaged you are with the real WHOM who is feeding you moment-by-moment clues in the WHERE.

After you find the keys, go back and recreate the "Hot and Cold" search to best of your recollection—without the keys and without the real WHOM. Instead, simply imagine both. Remember what you DID in the real circumstances, paying attention to the specific sensory details. Did you scan the bookshelf before you moved items? Did you laugh when the clues got "hotter and hotter?" Were the keys hard to reach behind the desk? Did you brush away the dust on the shelves? Be specific.

2. *Remember a setting you are familiar with. Describe the details out loud, even if a few of them are made up. It could be your bedroom, your backyard, the gym at school,*

or the view from you window at work. Fill the image with sensory details. Are there people in your WHERE? What season is it? What time of day? Describe other sensory details besides visual ones. Is the air crisp? Does the gym smell of sweat? Is the only sound in your room a ticking clock? Listen to the crowd in the last moments of a basketball game. Hear the rustle of the leaves on a fall day. Can you smell the smoke from the chimneys? The more specific the sensory details of the image, the better.

3. *On a daily basis, remind yourself to use your powers of self-observation. Take note the next time your hands feel sticky. How does it feel and how do you react to that feeling? What about your memory of and reaction to burned popcorn, the yapping bark of the neighbor's dog, the drip of a faucet, the look of a messy diaper? Make a list of sensory details you encounter throughout the day.*

For example:

Smell: *Old running shoes, honeysuckle on the porch, a new car, a campfire*

Taste: *Sour orange juice, bitter medicine, chocolate truffles*

Hearing: *School bells, speaker feedback, chirping birds, nails on a chalkboard*

Touch: *Velvet fabric, sandpaper, a sharp safety pin, playdough*

4. *Observe the sensory details in your kitchen. What do you see? Yes, it's a cabinet, but dig deeper. What does it look like? Is the paint peeling? Are the handles loose? Run your hand across the countertop. Is it full of crumbs? Is it sticky*

or squeaky-clean? Put your hands in the leftover dishwater. Is it warm or cold? Open the refrigerator. Does it smell like the fish from last night's dinner? Listen. Even a seemingly quiet house is full of sounds—a clock ticking, an airplane overhead, the footsteps from the upstairs' apartment. And what better place to experience "taste" than in the kitchen? Peel an orange and savor each juicy bite.

5. Remember the emotional reactions to the senses you experienced. Did you pick at the peeling paint on the cabinets in disgust? Did you grumble under your breath at the sticky honey on the countertops left by your roommate? Did the smell of baking bread make you smile? Did the ticking clock cause you to pick up the pace when you realized you were late for work?

> NOTE: Remember to include the WHEN with the WHERE. Is it so early there's barely any light in the room? Is it wintertime when the furnace never quite warms up the tile floor? Does the taste of a hot cup of coffee sound less appealing because it's 90 degrees at 8:00 am? Does bathing suit season affect how you feel about the sugar and other goodies in the kitchen?

6. Find a recording of a song that describes a place. "Oh, What a Beautiful Morning," "I Love Paris," or "Far From the Home I Love." (See the repertoire list at the end of the chapter for more examples.) As you listen to the music and the lyrics, imagine the visual details of an appropriate WHERE in the fourth wall. Add other sensory elements using touch, smell, taste, and hearing. Try this with country songs, pop songs, even nursery rhymes. The lyrics can provide useful information, and if they don't, you can fill out the imagery on your own.

7. Create a WHERE environment for a WHOM of your choice. Make sure that the WHOM is responding to the environment in your image. Is the child in your image frightened by the Halloween decorations in the yard? Are your lover's arms open as the wind rushes through her hair? Is your friend sweating as he changes his tire on the highway? How do their situations make you feel as an observer? Keep the action moving moment by moment.

8. Put yourself in the same environment as your WHOM. Do you respond the same way as your image? Are you laughing at the Halloween decorations that make your nephew cower? Does the wind irritate you as you try to keep your hair out of your face as you look into your lover's eyes? Are you freezing watching your friend change a tire as the sun goes down? Put yourself in a contrasting environment, such as watching your children make a snowman from your kitchen window.

9. Present an improvisation lecture on "How to Make an Ice Cream Sundae." Provide instruction to the following WHOMS in the following WHERES:

   • Business Colleagues
     In a business meeting at the office

   • Active and impatient kindergarteners
     On a picnic on a very hot day

   • To your devoted royal subjects
     At a ball in your honor

   • To a rowdy bunch of cowboys
     In a bar on a Saturday night

- *To a classroom of disinterested teens*
  In after-school detention

10. Start with your own WHERE, a place your character currently resides in. Describe the WHERE using sensory details in a made-up monologue. At some point in the monologue, "remember" something that happened before in a contrasting WHERE. Then, let your story return to the present WHERE or move on to a future WHERE. Provide each WHERE image with as many sensory details as you can think of. Let your eyes follow the scenery.

For example:

"I love coming here. The wheat is ready to harvest and my dad's tractor seat is a perfect perch. I can see my mother watering her flowers as my brother is working on his car. The barn needs painting and the chickens are madly competing for what little grain is left in the ground from their breakfast. The sun is hot today, and it makes me squint."

Here you recall another time and place.

"I've been thinking a lot about the way things were before were moved out here. It was so much fun having friends who lived within walking distance. **I remember** Andy and I would get up early and run down to the kitchen for a quick bite of pancakes and sausage. We would pool our money on the kitchen table and decide how much we could spend on candy at Mr. Palmer's filling station down the block. He had everything from licorice to wax lips to gold nugget bubblegum, all waiting for us in little boxes on the counter by the cash register. His place always smelled like gasoline and the floor

52

probably hadn't been swept in years, but it was the highlight of our week. I miss those years. It's not that I don't love the farm, but I miss the city. That's why I've made a decision."

Now you are imagining a future time and place.

*"I'm moving to Chicago in the fall. It's time for me to see the world and grow up a little. **I can just imagine** what it will be like—busy people determined to get where they're going and tall buildings that block the sun by late afternoon. There'll be cabs with loud horns, buses that blow their fumes in your face, but there will be ethnic food and musicians on every corner."*

A call of your mother's voice wakens you from your imagined WHERE. You return to your present WHERE.

"I guess I had better stop dreaming and get back to my chores."

Now, it's your turn. Use a setting you are familiar with in order to draw on the details of your present and past experiences, as well as your dreams for the future.

<u>WHERE/WHEN - Practice Repertoire</u>

At The Ballet   *(A Chorus Line)*
                                           M. Hamlisch/E. Kleban

Blame it on the Summer Night   *(Rags)* C. Strouse/
                                           S. Schwartz

Castle on a Cloud   *(Les Miserables)*
                                           C. M. Schonberg/A Boublil

Defying Gravity   (Wicked) *S. Schwartz*

Empty Chairs and Empty Tables   *(Les Miserables)*
                                           C.M. Schonberg/A. Boublil

Far From the Home I Love   *(Fiddler on the Roof)*
                                           J. Bock/S. Harnick

Good Morning Baltimore   *(Hairspray)* M. Shaiman/
                                           S. Wittman

I Love Paris   *(Can Can)* C. Porter

I Wanna Go Home   *(Avenue Q)* R. Lopez/J. Marx

I'm Dreaming of a White Christmas   Irving Berlin

I'm Flying   *(Peter Pan)* M. Charlap/
                                           C. Leigh

It's a Grand Night for Singing   *(State Fair)* R. Rodgers/
                                           O. Hammerstein

Lonely House   *(Street Scene)* K. Weill/
                                           L. Hughes

Memory   *(Cats)* A.L. Webber/
                                           T.S. Eliot

New York, New York	*(On the Town)* L. Bernstein/ B. Comden/A. Green
Night and Day	*(The Gay Divorcee)* C. Porter
Not for the Life of Me	*(Thoroughly Modern Millie)* J. Tesori/D. Scanlan
On the Street Where You Live	*(My Fair Lady)* A.J. Lerner/ F. Loewe
Standing on the Corner	*(The Most Happy Fella)* F. Loesser
Summertime	*(Porgy and Bess)* G. Gershwin/D. Heyward
The Autumn Leaves	J. Mercer/J. Kosma
The Kite	*(You're a Good Man, Charlie Brown)* C. Gesner
The Last Time I Saw Paris	J. Kern/O. Hammerstein
The Only Home I Know	*(Shenandoah)* G. Geld/ P. Udell
There are Giants in the Sky	*(Into the Woods)* S. Sondheim
What a Wonderful World	G.D. Weiss/B. Thiele
When You're Home in the Heights	*(In the Heights)* Un-Manuel Miranda
Who Will Buy	*(Oliver)* L. Bart
Wouldn't it be Loverly	*(My Fair Lady)* A.J. Lerner/ F. Loewe

Chapter 3

THE INNER IMAGE

Remember, Reflect, Pretend, Imagine

> *"Inner imagery is the thing that makes the audience plug into their own unconscious. Obviously they're not going to have the same inner imagery that you as an actor has, but because you have inner imagery, it releases theirs".*
> **Larry Moss**

The INNER IMAGE is what happens when you go inside of your head to remember a past event, a place, an object, or a person. It is reflective and reminiscent, but it might also be something you are contemplating for your future. It may also be the inner vision of your imagination with mystical ideas and fantastical possibilities. Because the INNER IMAGE only occurs in your mind, it will affect your visual focus. You will probably look askance rather than focusing your eyes on someone or something in the fourth wall. For example, your mom may recall your first day of kindergarten. At first, she will focus on you (the WHOM), but as she remembers the details in her mind's eye, her eyes will be unfocused, and she may look off into the distance. She will physically respond to this inner image, even though it may be in a subtle way.

When you respond to your INNER IMAGES, you will get a little lost in the moment, and you will tend to react less directly. It may be a faraway smile, a regretful shake of the head, or a subtle rolling of the eyes. When you reflect or remember, your hand gestures are also expressed in a less direct and energetic way, almost like a shadow of a once-upon-a-time or the possibility of a someday-maybe.

Your mom may smile a little as she recalls your embarrassed wave from the bus. She might even vaguely imitate her own wave as she explains the moment, or she might grimace a little as she recalls your choice of clothing for the day. Still in her own thoughts, her eyes may look slightly upward and outward as she thinks of the possibilities for your future but then down again when she feels the regret of not spending enough time with you. These inner moments, or INNER IMAGES, are an important part of our storytelling. They are generally used in conjunction with the outer images of the WHOM and the WHERE. Singers, in particular, have more opportunities for these inner moments due to the reflective nature of songs. As a singer, you will often be asked to stand alone on stage and express this inner world, a world that is best accessed through music and poetry.

> *"What a wee little part of a person's life are his acts and his words! His real life is led in his head, and is known to none but himself. All day long, the mill of his brain is grinding, and his thoughts, not those of other things, are his history."* **Mark Twain**

METHOD ACTING AND THE SINGER

This inner life of "I wonder," "I remember," "If only," "I wish," and "I hope" profoundly influences our motivations, our actions, and our attitudes. If you *wonder* how life would be with someone, you might be motivated to ask that particular someone out on a date. If you *remember* how badly someone treated you, you might angrily confront that person when he or she walks into a room. This inner-to-outer life is something you naturally do throughout your day, but it can be hard to fake when you must play someone else.

The technique called "Method Acting" encourages the actor to substitute his own emotional memories and reactions when playing a character. This can be especially helping when you must access your INNER IMAGES. For example, using your own feelings of elation on your wedding day might transfer to Eliza's joy in *My Fair Lady* when she recalls how she could have "danced all night." Although this method has been revised over the years to be less self-indulgent, it can be a little cumbersome if you are continually trying to substitute throughout a performance. This is especially an issue for singers who may not have time to access these feelings due to the timing restrictions and conditions of the music. Let's face it. As a singer, you basically have to jump on board a moving train. You must respond on time, in rhythm, and on pitch while still reflecting the musical underscore. Therefore, this process of substitution may be more helpful during the rehearsal process than in performance. In rehearsal, it might help you understand a character you might not otherwise relate to. If you do this while remaining true to the music, you can create a rich inner life, even when you're playing such epic characters as Evita or Jean Valjean.

> *"You must create the character's internal life...the thoughts, feelings, memories, and inner decisions that may not be spoken. When we look into the eyes of actors giving fully realized performances, we can see them thinking...that quality of nonverbal expression—which is as much a part of the characters as breathing and as real as what they say and do."* **Larry Moss**

> **Note:** If you close your eyes to better "see" the Inner Image, you will be shutting the audience out. Your audience wants to see you as you see the image. If your eyes remain closed, it's as if you're telling your audience, "I'm going away right now. I'll get back to you in a minute." This upsets the flow of the emotional information being shared. Granted, an angst-driven pop ballad may involve tightly shut eyes, but if it lasts for more than just a moment, the audience will feel cheated and ignored.

INNER TO OUTER/OUTER TO INNER

Your imagery informs your emotional life and inspires your physical reactions, but sometimes it works the other way around. The acting teacher, Constantin Stanislovsky, believed that, although imagery and inner feelings create expressive movement, expressive movement can also create an inner life of feeling as well. If you pound on a table long enough while shouting obscenities, it won't take long to connect with feelings of anger. If you crawl up into a ball and rock with your head in your hands, you may connect with feelings of despair. If you walk into an audition with a confident stride, even though you are nervous and unsure, some of that physical bravado may actually rub off on you.

> *"You're more likely to act yourself into feeling than feel yourself into action. So act!"*   **Samuel Smiles**

USING THE MUSIC FOR INSPIRATION

For the singer, the musical accompaniment will play an important role when it comes to your imagery and your reactions. It will not only inspire your inner life, but it will also tell you when the intent and the mood are changing. A driving beat followed by a sultry saxophone obviously signals a change of some kind, and that change can move you in a visceral way from anger to passion, depending on the content and context of the song. The point is this; the music, as well as the imagery, can create a feeling, evoke a memory, or inspire an action.

> **NOTE: The music can help you connect with the emotional life of a pirate king or a fairy godmother. It can also help you get in touch with your character's roots, whether you're an Arkansas country boy in *Big River*, an abandoned British orphan in *Oliver*, or a contemporary, New York Bohemian in *Rent.***

DON'T MISS THE POINT

Singers sometimes forget that singing, just like acting, is circular in nature. Instead, they think of it as a step-by-step process: 1. Set posture, 2. Inhale, 3. Engage support, 4. Exhale with tone, 5. Await judgment. It's so much more than that! Your air, your tone, your images, and your physical responses are the lifeblood of the inner to outer and back again world that expresses your soul.

EXERCISES

1. *In order to fill out the sensory details of your INNER IMAGERY, remember a life-changing moment in your life, perhaps a graduation, a break up with a girlfriend or boyfriend, or news of the death of a grandparent. Keep the time frame narrow in order to dig deeper rather than broader. Go through each of the senses and fill in sensory details surrounding the event to better remember it. For the actor, it is the small details that elicit emotional responses, not the vague conceptual ones, so dig into the specifics. For example, recall the details of picture-taking after graduation, your dad repairing your car, your little*

sister's tea parties, or one of your best friend's stupid practical jokes.

Try and visualize this moment without looking into the fourth wall. (Your eyes will probably have a faraway look if you are doing this correctly). Even though you are not including a fourth-wall WHOM or WHERE at this point, you may still find yourself smiling or weeping as you recall the event.

2. *Sometimes it's easier to access details when the events are more recent. Inside your head, without looking at images in the fourth wall, remember a recent, more insignificant event. For example, remember how you got ready for work or school this morning. Again, challenge yourself to remember sensory details. Remember moving your shirt hangers from side to side in order to find the yellow shirt you wanted to wear with your blue tie. Remember how it felt to pilfer through the cluttered drawer to find your mascara. Recall your wife or husband, mom or dad yelling up the steps for you to hurry up. Remember how you spilled orange juice on your shirt just as your impatient ride was honking the horn.*

3. *Watch documentaries where people must relate stories from their pasts. Watch what happens to their eyes when they go from speaking to the interviewer to "remembering" the event. You will notice that most people can talk with very little emotion when they are explaining things in broad terms, but when they move to the details in their INNER IMAGERY, they respond with far more emotion. Soldiers who relate war stories often hold up fine while they talk about body counts or battle strategy, but the minute they move to a specific inner moment--when they remember a PS in a letter or the sound of a deceased*

friend's laughter—their voices trail off and their eyes fill with tears.

4. *Rather than watch strangers, observe family members that you have a connection with tell stories from the past. Notice their INNER IMAGES, those moments when they go away to recall and gather emotional information. How do they respond to those memories? What are they remembering when they laugh aloud? What details in their stories make them roll their eyes or shake their heads? What inner details affect them the most?*

5. *Apply the principles of INNER IMAGERY to a song. Choose a reflective number that deals with memories from the past: "I Remember" by Sondheim, "It Was a Very Good Year" (a song made popular by Frank Sinatra), or "The Way We Were" (a song recorded by Barbra Streisand). Draw on specific memories from your own life as you listen to and/or sing the piece. (See suggested repertoire at the end of the chapter.)*

6. *Choose a song that allows you to create an INNER IMAGE based on "what will be" or "what could be," such as "Soliloquy" from Carousel, or "Wouldn't it Be Lovely" from My Fair Lady." Instead of a fixed look of longing, specifically imagine the details of what you're forecasting or hoping for. (See suggested repertoire at the end of the chapter.)*

7. *Cut out a variety of photos of individuals from various magazines. Avoid models in commercially "posed" pictures, and ignore the assigned captions. Briefly look at each photo and decide what each person is thinking or saying based on their face and body language. What is it about them that leads you to your answer? Then, decide on additional details. Who are they speaking to? Where are*

they going? Where have they been? What are the circumstances? Next, find a song that each person might be singing in the photo.

You can do a similar exercise while you're waiting in line or stuck in a large crowd. Observe people's actions and reactions, and then use your imagination. What are they thinking and feeling? What are their lives like? What song would suit their look and mood right now? It might be fun to do this with a friend and then compare your observations.

8. *Listen to orchestral music that is not associated with a story. Let yourself move freely to the phrasing and sonority. It's not about choreographed steps, but is, instead, an inner ballet that moves you to reach with outstretched arms or curl up in despair. Move your body in ways that reflect the beat, the rhythmic interplay, the mode, the melody, the tempo, the dynamics, and the orchestrations. Do the same exercise with a variety of instrumental styles, especially ones you aren't familiar with.*

NOTE: You can't avoid creative exercises because you feel awkward or embarrassed. There's simply no other way to learn to be an artist than through experimentation and experience. Oh, yes, and "failure." Without risk, you simply can't grow enough to be a successful performer. Reading about and analyzing "art" may make you a scholar, but it won't be enough to make you an artist.

INNER IMAGE – Practice Repertoire

All That's Known	*(Spring Awakening)* D. Sheik/S. Sater
A Quiet Thing	*(Flora, The Red Menace)* J. Kander/F.Ebb
Always on My Mind	Willie Nelson
Anyone Can Whistle	*(Anyone Can Whistle)* S. Sondheim
Anthem	*(Chess)* B. Andersson/ B. Ulvaeus/T. Rice
As Long as He Needs Me	*(Oliver)* L. Bart
Bring Him Home	*(Les Miserables)* C. M. Schonberg/ A. Boublil
Danny Boy	Frederic Weatherly
Days Gone By	*(She Loves Me)* J. Bock/S. Harnick
Disneyland	*(Smile)* M. Hamlisch/ H. Ashman
Empty Chairs and Empty Tables	*(Les Miserables)* C.M. Schonberg/ A. Boublil

Every Day a Little Death	*(A Little Night Music)* S. Sondheim
Far From the Home I Love	*(Fiddler on the Roof)* J. Bock
Goodnight My Someone	*(The Music Man)* M. Wilson
Hard Candy Christmas	*(The Best Little Whorehouse in Texas)* C. Hall
Home	*(The Wiz)* C. Smalls
I Could Have Danced All Night	*(My Fair Lady)* A.J. Lerner/ F. Loewe
I Don't Know How to Love Him	*(Jesus Christ Superstar)* A.L. Webber/T. Rice
If I Had Only Known	J. Stanfield/ C. Morris
I'm Not That Girl	*(Wicked)* S. Schwartz
I Remember	*(Evening Primrose)* S. Sondheim
I've Grown Accustomed to Her Face	*(My Fair Lady)* A.J. Lerner/F. Loewe
I'm Dreaming of a White Christmas	Irving Berlin
Mama a Rainbow	*(Minnie's Boys)* L. Grossman/ H. Hackady
Mama Look Sharp	*(1776)* S. Edwards

My Grandmother's Love Letters   Maury Yeston

Once Upon a December   *(Anatasia)*
L. Ahrens/S. Flaherty

Once Upon a Time   *(All American)*
C. Strouse/Lee Adams

On My Way to You   A. & M. Bergman

Reflection   *(Mulan)* J. Goldsmith

Santa Fe   *(Newsies)*
A. Menken/
J. Feldman

Sorry Grateful   *(Company)*
S. Sondheim

The Only Home I Know   *(Shenandoah)*
G. Geld/P. Udell

What is a Woman?   *(I Do, I Do)*
H. Schmidt/T. Jones

What More Can I Say   *(Falsettos)* W. Finn

When She Loved Me   *(Toy Story)*
R. Newman

Where Do You Start   J. Mandel/
A. & M. Bergman

Where I Want to Be   *(Chess)*
B. Andersson/
B Ulvaeus/T. Rice

Yesterday   Paul McCartney

Chapter 4

MOVING FROM IMAGE TO IMAGE

The Journey of the Mind and Body

When you watch people tell stories, you will notice that they continually move from image to image. They intermittently speak to their WHOM, respond to the WHERE, and look askance to remember the INNER IMAGES. One moment affects the next, and the one after that, and the one after that.

Moving from image to image is of great importance to the actor. This is because, in real life, it's generally an emotional connection that causes you to move from one image to another. Even when your WHOM is initially your focus, you may need to move to INNER IMAGERY to remember an important detail to share. Conversely, the INNER IMAGE may become so vivid and vital, that you must share it with your WHOM.

THE IMPORTANCE OF PLAY

As you have already learned, to be an effective performer you must feed your images with strong sensory details. When you choose strong details for your images, you will react to these details physically. When you react physically, you begin to build a sensory and emotional atmosphere that will spark even more creative ideas and images. After a while, you may not even need to invent details. They will just flow out of you, and, before you know it, you will simply be going along for the ride, naturally moving from image to image. In other words, you will play make believe. Hopefully, you did this as a child. You would decide on a character ("I'll be a king"), a WHOM ("My make-believe friend will be my knight."), and a WHERE ("We're preparing for battle in front of an abandoned castle"—that just happens to look a lot like the garage.) You probably didn't have to work very hard on subsequent details, and your INNER IMAGES were probably thoughts that propelled you into a storyline. The imagery simply flowed through you as you experienced the story moment by moment...until it was time for dinner.

> *"When I examine myself and my methods of thought, I come to the conclusion that the gift of fantasy has meant more to me than any talent for abstract, positive thinking."*   *Albert Einstein*

NOTE: Today's children are often micro-managed with adult-driven activities rather than being encouraged to "go out and play." Playtime is when children are challenged to use their imaginations and make creative choices. Nothing in life can be invented, discovered, or developed without imagination and creative choices. Play is, in fact, a highly productive activity!

For the singing actor, there must be a balance between the free flow of feeling that naturally moves your images, and the tools and techniques that lead you to make imagery choices. The script, the lyrics, and the musical accompaniment will all influence these choices. This chicken-and-egg cycle can be a little confusing, so, at this point, it's important to let the following material in this chapter wash over you. Apply the principles using the exercises provided, but remember that these are guidelines for a process, not rules for a pre-determined outcome. It all may seem a little less convoluted if you simply remember that IMAGERY is something you do naturally every day. Your job, as a performer, is to learn how to harness it to serve your artistic purposes.

> *"I chose and my world was shaken. So what? The choice may have been mistaken; the choosing was not."*
> *Stephen Sondheim*

DECIDING WHEN AND WHY

The music, the lyrics, and/or the script will certainly inform your choices when it comes to imagery, helping you decide what images to use where in order to heighten the artistic impact of the performance. This probably means that you will move to an image when the music or lyrics call for it. Sometimes, however you will simply move from image to image when you are emotionally compelled to do so. Your images may also change due to a simple stream of consciousness. For example, when you daydream about your daughter being valedictorian, you may suddenly remember to tell your husband he must pick her up from school.

Sometimes the INNER IMAGE may become so vivid, you will need to move it into the fourth wall to share it with your WHOM. You do this constantly throughout your day without being aware of it. For example, as you use an INNER IMAGE to recall the game where you were tackled by a monster linebacker, the need to explain his stature to your WHOM may momentarily cause you to move his image into the fourth wall, where you will vaguely outline the size of his shoulders with your hands. If you are recalling a WHERE, the sensory memories may grow until you will begin to faintly "see" the location of various images in the fourth wall—the general store on your left, the old Presbyterian Church on your right, and the field of buttercups on the mountain behind them.

THE BALLET OF MOVING IMAGES

Throughout your day, notice the ballet between your WHOM, your WHERE, and your INNER IMAGES. You must ask yourself what it is that changes the image. Is it a stream of consciousness that reminds you of something else? Is it a vivid sensory memory that must live in the fourth wall? Or, is it an outside force that changes your focus? Musical theatre and opera selections are often long monologues with a vivid flow of images. This is why it's as important to practice your imagery as it is to practice your scales and arpeggios.

AN EXAMPLE OF MOVING IMAGES

> **CIRCUMSTANCES:** You are at the airport to pick up a friend, but you're not quite sure you're in the right place at the right time.

> **WHERE:** You are looking around the baggage claim area taking in all of the scenery that surrounds you. You see the conveyer belt to your left with people waiting for their luggage. On the right, there is a staircase that your friend will eventually descend to claim her baggage. You see limo drivers holding signs and people happily greeting each other. You suddenly feel something tugging at your coat.

> **WHOM:** You look down and see a little girl holding your coat with one hand and holding a dripping ice

cream cone in the other. You smile, until she gives you a dirty look, followed by a raspberry. Your smile turns to shock as the little girl wipes her hands on your coat.

A SECOND WHOM: You look to her mother for help. The mother apologizes to you and pulls the little girl away.

A THIRD WHOM: Just as you are checking your coat for ice cream stains, an elderly lady walks by and asks for the time. You tell her, but that reminds you that you're not sure of your friend's arrival time.

INNER: You struggle to recall the previous night's phone conversation with your friend. She said something about having lunch, so it had to be before noon. On the other hand, she lives in a different time zone...

WHERE: You look around to see if there is a arrival board that will give you a clue, but, as you do, you begin to question if this is actually the same terminal you picked her up in last time. It seems like the same one, yet there are things that are different than you remember.

INNER: You again try and recall yesterday's phone conversation with your friend when she mentioned the airline and the arrival time. You remember other tidbits of conversation, but can't recall the details of her flight.

WHERE: You decide that you definitely need to find the flight board. You look around for it until you notice a few people studying it to your left. The lettering is small, so you move closer to get a better look. The arrival information is confusing and that frustrates you.

INNER: Now, you begin to question what airline she's on. "I should have been paying attention. Did she say Southwest or Delta? Oh no, what if she's already arrived and waiting for me in another terminal?"

WHERE: You begin to search the crowd, but now you're really worried. As you scan the baggage area one more time, you squint to make out an image that looks like your friend way in the back of the claim area. She walks a little closer, and you see her waving to you. You wave back.

INNER: You take a breath, briefly thinking about what you've put yourself through the last 15 minutes.

WHOM: As she draws closer, you continue waving and smiling. When you meet, however, her angry complaints about the nightmare of a flight she's just experienced make you wonder if it was all worth it. (Ah, the active image!)

NOTE: Acting isn't a matter of classifying and setting the **WHOM**, the **WHERE**, and the **INNER IMAGES**. It's more important to experience them, change them, and embellish them until you achieve a desired outcome. When you do the same role night after night, or when you use the same audition piece over and over, it's important to make changes to keep your reactions fresh, as if they are spontaneous and happening for the first time.

EXERCISES

1. *Decide on a WHOM, WHEN, WHERE, and a set of CIRCUMSTANCES. Carve out about two minutes of action. Fill in the moment-to-moment details in your mind. Act out the whole scene in **slow motion**. (The dialogue should silently be mouthed.) Notice how your imagery changes from moment to moment—from the WHOM, to your INNER IMAGES, to a WHERE. This slow motion moment-by-moment action will not only make you aware of your reactions, it will remind you of where and why your imagery moves.*

2. *Use a room of your house that you can freely walk through. Create an imaginary WHERE for the space. (For example, your living room could be a science lab). Take a WHOM image of your choice on a tour of your imaginary WHERE, explaining the entire facility and all of the "imaginary" items in the space. Occasionally, stop and reflect on the past or imagine your hopes for the future (INNER IMAGES). Return to the WHOM and WHERE throughout the exercise.*

3. *After you have recreated a scenario in Exercise 2, practice singing the "tour" on "la". You can use a tune you know, but the actual lyrics are irrelevant. Notice how the imagery affects your voice throughout the entire scene. Even though there are no words, if you are internally saying, "Oh, no, where did that come from?" your inflection will reflect this comment. Your imagery will not only affect your voice, but your gestures as well. ("Don't touch that. It could explode."), and your facial expressions ("Why are you looking at me like that?").*

Note: Although your speaking voice will be profoundly affected by your imagery and emotional life, your singing voice may have more limitations. Some styles will allow you to adjust your dynamics, hesitate on a particular word, or over-articulate a certain consonant, and some won't. Even if you are working with limitations, remember that your voice must reflect the feeling. Think of the vocal contrast between singing a prayer for a loved one and singing a song of angry protest. ("Bring Him Home" versus "Do You Hear the People Sing")

4. *Focus primarily on a WHERE as you sing (on "la") the melody of "Twinkle, Twinkle" or "Happy Birthday." Make up your own scenes to continue developing your imagination.*

Notice the details in the following example:

WHERE: *Imagine yourself standing at the edge of the Grand Canyon. Shout out the "la" song loudly enough to produce an echo that comes from the far side of the canyon walls. It's fun, so you smile at your own antics. You continue looking around (into that fourth wall). Below, you wave to a party of tourists riding donkeys, and they wave back. You inhale deeply and smell the sage mixed with the Italian sausages the people next to you are enjoying as they also enjoy the view. You smile politely, wishing you had one of those sausages but the gentle breeze and warm sunshine reminds you how lucky you are to have this moment.*

Notice how the images affect the vocal tone and volume, as well as your facial expressions and body language.

5. *Primarily focus on a WHOM as you sing using the same process as Exercise #4.*

Notice the details in the following example:

WHOM: *You're talking (singing) to your best friend in the lobby of a hotel, explaining how upset you are over your recent breakup. As you relate the details, you notice your ex has just walked into the lobby, and he (or she) is talking intimately with a person you've never met. (You are now speaking/singing in a hushed tone). Your jealousy gets the best of you. Now move your WHOM image from your friend to your ex. Your voice should reflect the anger you are feeling.*

Even though YOU are the only one on stage, the situation and the images are reflected in your body and your voice.

6. *Primarily focus on an INNER IMAGE as you sing using the same process as in Exercise #4.*

   Notice the details in the following example:

   Remember receiving a favorite childhood present. Remember when you received it and where. Think about the fun or the affection you felt as you played with it or cuddled it. Remember the joy on the face of the one who gave it to you. Think about what happened to the gift. Is it still on the shelf? Did you give it away? Let the fond memories return in an intimate, internal way. As you sing, notice the reflective quality in your voice.

7. *Now that you've practiced creating details for the WHOM, the WHERE, and in your INNER IMAGES, practice moving from image to image in scenes that require you to do so quickly. Speak a running monologue out loud to keep yourself on track, almost like you're dubbing your thoughts into a movie.*

An example of the spoken monologue as you experience the rapid fire images:

(CIRCUMSTANCES: Black Friday. It's midnight, and they are getting ready to open the doors to the mall. One shopper keeps cutting in line.)

"I can't believe I've been here for the last three hours. I remember falling asleep around 8:00, or at least I think I did. Oh, wait, they're getting ready to open the doors. Oh, no, what's this woman doing? She's trying to get in front of me. Hey, lady. Wait your turn! What's all the noise? Oh, here comes the security officer. It's time. What? We have to wait another 10 minutes? This is the last time I come here. I remember last year when we had to wait an hour. Hey, stop pushing"...etc.

Other scenes that might involve moving quickly from image to image:

- *You are the substitute teacher for an unruly class of hyper kindergarteners. You are trying to impress the principal who is visiting your classroom so you can get hired at the school.*
- *You are on a paintball course with your boyfriend and his ex-girlfriend. She is seeking revenge.*

Come up with a few of your own scenes based on your own life experiences.

8. *Sometimes it's difficult to find adults with larger-than-life imaginations, so offer to babysit a niece, a nephew, or a friend's child. Engage in an evening of make-believe. Watch the child point out the WHOM, the WHERE, and the WHEN, as well as the circumstances, as you play pretend. Especially be aware of the child's inner life, his or her*

INNER IMAGES. (This usually occurs right before the child says, "I know what we can do!")

9. *As mentioned earlier, use imagery while practicing your vocal exercises. For example, if you are singing on a "mi," selfishly tell your WHOM, "It's all about me!" If you are performing scales on a lyrical "ah," look at a tranquil WHERE scene. "Ne, nay, nah, no, noo" can be used to scold your child for misbehavior. This will reinforce the connection between your voice and your acting, but it will also shut down judgmental inhibitors that sometimes make you vocally uptight. Putting your sound "out there" with an image may even relax your voice and kick in your breath support.*

NOTE: Sometimes the imagery takes a back seat when a song is more visceral in nature. Although you still may want to use imagery to establish a mood, sometimes it's enough to simply feel the sensuality of a jazz scat riff or the anger in a driving metal up-tempo. Songs can be "celebration" or "rage" or raw "sexuality" depending on the style. Sometimes, a song is more about the dance moves (disco), or the rhythm in the words (rap) than the imagery. Sometimes the voice is simply another instrument in the ensemble, mimicking an improvising clarinet or the distorted sound of a heavy metal guitar.

MOVING THE IMAGE – Practice Repertoire

Use the repertoire listed in previous chapters to practice moving from image to image. Remember to continually respond to your ACTIVE IMAGES.

Chapter 5

WHAT DO I DO WITH MY HANDS?

"No, really. What *do* I do with my hands?"

"A poem in form still has to have voice, a gesture, a sense of discovery, a metaphoric connection, as any poetry does."   *Robert Morgan*

The answer to "What do I do with my hands?" is ... (drum roll) "nothing." Okay, you deserve a better answer, but if you have read the previous chapters, you will have begun to understand that your attention won't be on your hands. It will be on the imagery. If you are truly engaged in your images, your hands will most likely respond naturally. Unmotivated gestures that are not connected to your images take the focus away from your face, and your face is what the audience is interested in. Dancers will be the first to tell you that the audience often looks at the face rather than the fancy footwork. It's simply better to initially sing with neutral hands that are relaxed at your side rather than producing a "singer posture." The one-hand-on-the-piano approach many singers use is, in itself, an unnatural expression, and the cupped hands at belly level are cliché and affected.

STARTING IN NEUTRAL

If you are engaged in your image, you will naturally reach out, reach for, point out, or push away. From a neutral

81

hands-at-your-side position, you will be more likely to move your hands only when emotionally motivated to do so. This will also keep you from those distracting nervous habits, like pushing your hair out of your eyes (a big no-no!) or wringing your hands. You will also need to be aware of the dreaded upward palms, which a singer substitutes for "anything" emotional when, in real life, the gesture is only used for receiving change.

Does this mean you don't move your hands? Of course not. Your hands are the natural connection to your words, and when the gestures are connected to the imagery, the hands are a natural way to communicate. If, however, your hands are manufactured in an indicating way, they are only distractions. Plus, the rest of your body will give you away if you try and choreograph a gesture. For example, if your hands are on your hips to "indicate" confidence, but your feet are shuffling and your shoulders are hunched, your audience simply won't buy it.

> *"Every word, facial expression, gesture, or action on the part of a parent gives the child some message about self-worth."* **Virginia Satir**

INDICATING—JUST SAY "NO."

Folding your hands together, pointing one toe, and batting your eyelashes may be fine for a parody, but it doesn't honestly express being in love. If your assignment is to sing to your forlorn little puppy who is being scolded for peeing on the floor, don't mime petting him while you stick out your lower lip to "indicate" pity. Certain "indications" are acceptable—tapping your watch to stress to your friend that he's late, or "strangling someone" with your hands to express frustration and anger—but these gestures come from a truthful place that is an outgrowth of feeling, not a secret code for guessing.

NOTE: Children's theatre classes can be great fun, but they can also reinforce some bad habits. When children are only given "monkey-see, monkey-do" gestures that don't connect to the story or the music, they may become disengaged performers. Thus, there must be a balance between the outward expression and the inward motivation. A pair of snazzy jazz hands are fine, but if those hands don't connect with a "Wow, we did it!" or a "pure joy of living" feeling, they become empty clichés. Teaching this connection is worth so much more to a child than putting him or her on stage in an overpriced costume with a set of cute moves.

GESTURES – NATURAL / CHOREOGRAPHED

As you've learned, the human body is too complex to fake a response that doesn't include an emotionally connected image. In real life, when you are angrily screaming at your lover the moment he or she walks out the door, your whole body kicks in. Your center may shift, your knees may lock, your hands may clinch, and your eyes may squint. Yet, this moment will fly by so fast that taking an inventory of physical responses and re-creating them will simply be impossible, especially when, in the next second, the focus of your scorn starts crying and asking for your forgiveness. Instead, focus on your imagery, and, if you must create a move, try and remember how you felt and how you reacted when you were once in that particular situation.

"No art is any good unless you can feel how it's put together. By and large it's the eye, the hand and if it's any good, you feel the body. Most of the best stuff seems to be a complete gesture, the totality of the artist's body."
                                                                    Frank Stella

---

83

OBSERVATION

The best way to study "sincere" versus "insincere" body language is to watch television spokespeople, newscasters, preachers, and politicians. When one of these people seems insincere, it's probably due to disconnected gestures and fixed stares that have no imagery. A minister looking down at notes while opening up his or her arms to "embrace" the congregation will not be nearly as effective as the minister who looks out to the flock with open arms. Watch a few so-called reality series on television. It's usually pretty obvious when the participants are being genuine and when they are speaking from a script, usually because they are usually lousy "actors." Ask yourself why they look so unnatural and awkward. Where are their eyes? Are their images moving? Are the gestures connected to the images? On the other hand, beware of the lying politician who has mastered imagery and body language. Sometimes the villain may be wearing a white hat, full of "sincere" rhetoric and "honest" moves.

> *"We see that every external motion, act, gesture, whether voluntary or mechanical, organic or mental, is produced and preceded by internal feeling or emotion, will or volition, and thought or mind."*   *H. P. Blavatsky*

THE TIMING OF THE GESTURE

The biggest mistake singers make is the timing of a gesture because they forget an important truth; we see something *before* we respond to it (unless we are reacting viscerally after "Boo!" or "Watch out!") That's why gestures that occur on the first beat of a musical phrase rarely ring true. Musical introductions and interludes are vital to your acting because they supply that "moment before" your reaction. Whatever occurs in this moment generally compels you to sing and act a certain way. If you are simply clearing your throat, watching the accompanist, or seating your breath during these "before" and "between" musical moments, you are missing an important emotional connection. The music that accompanies the "moment before" is important to you, and, if you're lucky, the composer will inspire your acting choices with a rich and informative accompaniment. If not, it's your job to fill these moments with engaging imagery.

> **NOTE: Why is it people use their hands when they're talking on the phone? Why do voice-over actors still physically express the lines when it's only their voices that will be heard? It's because we innately connect our actions and our words. We express feeling through our hands and our voices in tandem. That's why learning a song and then trying to add "actions" later usually doesn't work.**

OTHER BENEFITS OF IMAGERY

There are other benefits of imagery besides effective acting and natural gestures. For one thing, you're less likely to let nerves take over if you're engaged in the image, the fantasy, and the moment. In fact, if your nerves get the best of you, instead of feeling as if you are standing there being judged, think of making your performance more expressive, more connected to your imagery.

Memorizing lines and lyrics like a grocery list in the informational left-brain tends to disconnect the emotional response of the more intuitive right brain. Therefore, you are also more likely to remember lyrics if they are connected to visual images that are unfolding one to the next. (Studies have shown that the best reading comprehension occurs when the reader can visualize as he or she reads.) And, of course, as mentioned earlier, strong imagery will also help you do away with those nervous habits that distract from your performance—twirling your hair, picking at your trousers, shuffling your feet, and pushing your hair out of your eyes.

Imagery can also help you release the tone and fill the room with your sound without pushing on your vocal cords. Think about it. When you are emotionally engaged, you breath is engaged, and the breath is what elevates the speaking voice into the singing voice. Breath is the motor behind the voice that elevates speech to a higher realm.

MAKING CHOREOGRAPHY WORK

As a performer, you will be given choreography for various lyrics, whether you are in a musical theatre production or singing in a Motown group. It's your job to connect these moves emotionally to an image. If you are choreographed to reach out on the line, "I need you," it's important to reach for someone or something. If you are singing, "Stop in the name of love," you should be stopping someone or something. It's up to you to make the choreography work theatrically.

"Behold the hands, how they promise, conjure, appeal, menace, pray supplicate, refuse, beckon, interrogate, admire, confess, cringe, instruct, command, mock and what not besides, with a variation and multiplication of variation which makes the tongue envious."
                                                            Michel de Montaigne

---

ON THE SPOT

Although it can be valuable to write down specific imagery details, like the WHOM's height or the scenery details in the WHERE, it is even better to come up with these elements in a more spontaneous, on-the-spot way, especially if you want to emotionally connect your imagery and your gestures. You will rarely have time to sit and contemplate while acting anyway. Your scene partner may suddenly react with anger rather than annoyance, or the director may decide on an entirely new interpretation, so you must be able to toss the ball back without taking the time to write a research paper. Be ready to react to anything and deny nothing.

There's nothing wrong with writing down your ideas since it will activate the intellectual side of your brain. However, it also might shut down the emotional, sensory, and improvisational side of your brain if you aren't careful. Acting is a different kind of study than most of your college academics. As an actor, multiple choice and true-and-false exams will get you nowhere. Instead, you must develop the improvisational, intuitive, and imaginative child you left behind a long time ago. Since acting has to happen on the spot, you must also get past your fears and inhibitions. Basically, if you are going to pursue theatre, you must invite your inner child to come out and play! With this in mind, don't be afraid to make changes and try new things during the rehearsal process. There is no failure—just choices, and stronger choices. An author may start with a thesis, but as he or she writes, new ideas and images will emerge, things not considered earlier. It's the process that reveals the truth for the writer or the performer. There will always be a stronger choice. You just have to look for it.

> *"Every child is an artist. The problem is how to remain an artist once we grow up."*　　　　　**Pablo Picasso**

EXERCISES

1. *Select a song from repertoire in the previous chapters or from your own personal repertoire. Take a look at the first line of the song, and the subsequent lines that occur after interludes. What is it you see (or hear and feel) right before the line? Use the tools of imagery (WHOM, WHERE, WHEN, and INNER IMAGES) to inform your choices. What did you see before you opened your arms up to a new day in "Oh, What a Beautiful Morning?" What did your boyfriend do that made you angry enough to sing the line, "I hate men"? What "moment before" made you decide to "wash that man right out of your hair?" Notice how natural your gestures are when you have a reason to sing or speak.*

2. *Use your hands to smear imaginary paint all over the empty space in the room. Pretend to pick up small specks of glitter gently falling from the sky. Once you have gathered enough glitter throw it in the air as if you are casting a spell. Push aside the air in front of you as if it were the consistency of Jello. Then, using the same motions, cast an evil spell. (There are plenty of musicals that require the casting of spells.) Continue connecting your images to your hands. Reach for the highest spot in the room without the benefit of a chair or ladder. Reach for the furthest image you can see out of a window without moving your feet. (Sometimes this physical "reach" can also be the metaphorical "reaching" for love or hope in a song.) Don't forget to see the images!*

3. *Pretend to take imaginary miniature set pieces out of an imaginary toy box, and build a tiny invisible set. Make sure*

your eyes and hands work together as you move each piece into place. For example, create the campsite for a safari. Open the flap on the tent you have placed in the center of your set. Place a cot, table, and lantern inside the tent, paying attention to their relative size and location. Place small trees around the campsite and then place a tiger behind the trees. Add a table with provisions, and then, add the action figure who is camping in the brush. Notice how little you worry about your hands when they are engaged in a visual purpose.

4. *Speak the following phrases with your hands at your side.*

"Please come back!"

"I promise I'll never do that again."

"What are you doing here?"

"Oh, no! Don't touch that."

"Quiet. We're going to get caught."

"Get over here. Now!"

"I've had enough!"

"It was this little bitty kitten."

"Stop touching me."

"You're the best mom in the whole, wide world."

Now, include a strong WHOM image along with a reason for saying each phrase. Let your hands move naturally this time.

5. *Sing the phrases in Exercise #4. Make up the tune, but sing the lines as if they are lyrics. Practice it with your hands at your side, and then allow your hands to move naturally as you repeat the phrase a number of times. Remember that your voice must reflect the intention of the phrase as well.*

6. *Practice reprimanding someone you despise. Keep your hands at your side until you absolutely can't keep them there any longer. (Musical example: "Just You Wait, Henry Higgins.")*

7. *Study television commercials. Note the imagery and the gestures of various spokespeople. Do they look straight into the camera without drawing on inner images? Do they look at the product as they gesture? Are their hands natural or awkward? Determine what it is about their body language and imagery that makes them engaging, or not.*

8. *Watch people who are on the phone as they listen and respond to what is being said on the other end. What can you gather from the conversation based on their body language? Is it a dreaded call? Are they hanging on every word, or are they bored and distracted? Turn off the sound of the television to observe body language as well.*

Watch people discussing something at a restaurant, especially when you can't hear their conversation. Imagine what they are discussing based on their physical reactions. Notice how much emotional information can be acquired by simply watching body language and facial expressions. (Watch the movie, Date Night when the lead characters sit in a restaurant and interpret the conversations at various tables.)

9. *Sing something simple on "la", such as "Twinkle Twinkle" (Lyrics are irrelevant for this exercise). Without forcing the gestures, sing it with the following objectives:*

   You are giving something to someone as you sing, such as a gift, or a food item. The WHOM refuses it. Notice what happens to your hands when you:

   - *Encourage them to take.*
   - *Insist that they take it.*
   - *Force them to take it.*
   - *Tease them into accepting it.*

10. *Continue singing on "la" or speak a repeated nonsense word as you try the following exercises. Make a strong choice when it comes to the WHOM and the WHERE.*

    - *Try to get someone who is sad to laugh. (They aren't amused, but you are willing to do anything to get them to respond.) Consider how your WHOM and WHERE will affect your choices. For example, you might be more willing to go over-the-top at a party than at a place of worship.*

    - *Attempt to "shush" a noisy crowd of family members, a mob at a riot, or a group of partying friends. What happens to your hands and your voice? What changes when you choose a different WHOM, WHERE, or WHEN?*

    - *You are a cheerleader. Try and get the crowd excited during a boring, uneventful game. Don't just*

*use typical cheerleader moves. Instead, really focus
on the response, or lack thereof, of the crowd.*

- *Motivate a couch potato to get off the sofa to go for
a run with you. First ask, then plead, then bribe, and
finally, threaten.*

MOTIVATED MOVEMENT - Practice Repertoire

A Call from the Vatican	*(Nine)* M. Yeston
All That Jazz	*(Chicago)* J. Kander/F. Ebb
Art is Calling for Me	*(The Enchantress)* V. Herbert
Big Spender	*(Sweet Charity)* C. Coleman/D. Fields
Blow Gabriel Blow	*(Anything Goes)* C. Porter
Born to Hand Jive	*(Grease)* J. Jacobs/ W. Casey
Ease on Down the Road	*(The Wiz)* C. Smalls
Easy Street	*(Annie)* C. Strouse/ M. Charmins
Footloose	*(Footloose)* K. Loggins
Get Me to the Church on Time	*(My Fair* Lady) A.J. Lerner/F. Loewe
Greased Lightning	*(Grease)* J. Jacobs/ W. Casey
Guys and Dolls	*(Guys and Dolls)* F. Loesser
Honey Bun	*(South Pacific)* R. Rodgers/ O. Hammerstein

I am a Pirate King	*(The Pirates of Penzance)* W.S. Gilbert/A. Sullivan
I'm a Yankee Doodle Dandy	*(George M.)* G. M. Cohen
I Know Things Now	*(Into the Woods)* S. Sondheim
I'm in Love with a Wonderful Guy	*(South Pacific)* R. Rodgers/ O. Hammerstein
I'm Not at All in Love	*(The Pajama Game)* R. Adler/J. Ross.
I Shall Marry the Miller's Son	*(A Little Night Music)* S. Sondheim
It Don't Mean a Thing	D. Ellington/I. MIlls
I've Gotta Crow	*(Peter Pan)* M. Charlap/C. Leigh
Moving Too Fast	*(The Last Five Years)*-J.R. Brown
New York New York	*(On the Town)* L. Bernstein/ B. Comden/A. Green
No Bad News	*(The Wiz)* C. Small
Ooh, My Feet	*(The Most Happy Fella)* F. Loesser
Sit Down, You're Rockin' the Boat	*(Guys and Dolls)* F. Loesser

Slap That Bass	G. Gershwin/ I. Gershwin
Slide Some Oil	*(The Wiz)* C. Small
Show Off	(*The Drowsy Chaperone*) L. Lambert/ G. Morrison
Razzle Dazzle	*(Chicago)* J. Kander/ F. Ebb
Run and Tell That	*(Hairspray)* M. Shaiman/ S. Wittman
Sadder But Wiser Girl	*(The Music Man)* M. Wilson
There is a Sucker Born Every Minute	*(Barnum)* C. Coleman/ M. Stewart
To Life	*(Fiddler on the Roof)* J. Bock/S. Harnick
Whatever Lola Wants	*(Damn Yankees)* R. Adler/J. Ross
Wonder of Wonders	*(Fidder on the Roof)* J. Bock/S. Harnick
Young and Healthy	*(42nd Street)* H. Warren/A. Dubin
You Can't Stop the Beat	*(Hairspray)* M. Shaiman/ S. Wittman

Chapter 6

SUBSTITUTION AND BORROWING

Yours, Mine, and Ours

"Acting is not about being someone different, it's finding the similarity in what is apparently different, then finding myself in there."　　　　　　　　　　*Meryl Streep*

SUBSTITUTION

You talk and act differently at home than you do at work, a ballgame, or a cocktail party. Are you "being yourself" in each of these environments? Sure, but then again, there are many different versions of *you.* If you are aware of these varied personalities, you can probably SUBSTITUTE pieces of your own character for the characters you play on stage. If you are, for example, a high-strung person who must play someone more reserved and sophisticated, you might want to substitute your usual frenetic energy for the reserved persona you display at a job interview or at your grandmother's formal dinners.

Directors have been known to ask child actors to SUBSTITUTE the loss of their own pet or loved one to get the child to cry in a sad scene--pretty cruel trick. However, it does illustrate the acting technique of SUBSTITUTION. Taken to an extreme, it can get messy and confusing if you are trying to constantly substitute one part of your life for another, but it is helpful if you need to draw on something you know to understand something you don't know. For example, if you are required to sing a tender love song, but have never been in love, it might be okay to SUBTSTITUTE the love you have for a pet or an endearing grandparent. If you are having trouble singing the lyric, "Smile though your heart is breaking" with sincerity to an adult, it may be less complicated and more tender if you sing it to a small child or pet as well. The audience won't know what your image is. They will simply love the sincerity of the delivery.

You can also SUBSTITUTE your own experiences to fill out the scenery in your fourth wall. If you're singing, "the hills are alive" in the *Sound of Music,* you don't necessarily have to imagine the Austrian Alps designated in the script. You may have your own image of the Colorado Rockies you saw on vacation with your family, or you may even draw on the awe you felt the first time you saw the size of the new football stadium in town. Again, the audience doesn't care what your image is. They just want to see your response to it. If those images make you feel the same way Maria does when she surveys the Alps, that's all that matters.

"You have to get beyond your own precious inner experiences. The actor cannot afford to look only to his own life for all his material nor pull strictly from his own experience to find his acting choices and feelings. The ideas of the great playwrights are almost always larger than the experiences of even the best actors."

Stella Adler

BORROWING AND OBSERVATION

Sometimes we have to resort to BORROWING the characteristics of someone else. Think of it as borrowing a cup of sugar from a neighbor to complete a recipe you already have most of the ingredients for. If you are a shy person who must play a rowdy party animal, but you have few life experiences that will help you out, you may want to BORROW the look and attitudes of your sister's boyfriend, the drummer in a heavy metal band who knows how to have a good time. BORROWING requires OBSERVATION. Actors must continually observe others, and once they do, they must practice borrowing their postures, their walks, their voices, their attitudes, and their energy. You might even find yourself borrowing traits from various animals, such as the waddle of a duck for a frumpy old school teacher, or the slow, deliberate moves of a sloth in order to play a lazy couch potato.

EXPERIENCE AND IMAGINATION

Your best acting will occur when your imagination and your actual experiences converge. If you've never known a pirate before, it might seem daunting to play one. However, there's plenty of places to go for ideas. You can borrow the moves, the looks, and the physical expression of a pirate from movies, books, *and* real life. For example, you can watch *Pirates of the Caribbean,* read *Treasure Island,* or base the pirate's personality on your Uncle Larry, with his gruff voice, boisterous laugh, and devil-may-care attitude. Although these outer references will supplement and enhance your imagery, your own personality must still come through as you sing, "I am a Pirate King" from the *Pirates of Penzance.* This will also assure that the pirate is a character and not a caricature.

> *"Acting is a question of absorbing other people's personalities and adding some of your own experience."*
> *Jean-Paul Sartre*

WHAT IF

Opera and musical theatre performers often play characters with over-the-top personalities in larger-than-life situations. Where it may be fairly reasonable to conjure up a WHOM, WHERE, and WHEN for these characters, it may be more challenging to imagine and respond to their inner lives when you have little in common with them. Sometimes, when the character has little you can identify with, you may simply have to use your imagination and ask yourself, "WHAT IF?" What if I was the general in a Civil War battle? (This, of course, might require a little bit of homework.) What if I was the principal of the school instead of a student? What if I lived in fear of losing my home (as in Anatevka in *Fiddler on the Roof)?*

> *"I believe in imagination. I did Kramer vs. Kramer before I had children. But the mother I would be was already inside of me."*
> *Meryl Streep*

What if I was a mother? What if I was a mother who had been turned into a teapot? What if I was a mother who had been turned into a teapot and had to raise a teacup for a child? What if I had to be and do all of this while living under the roof of a temperamental beast? Basically, you must take what you already know and then ask yourself, "What would I do if I were in the same situation as this character?"

> *"With any part you play, there is a certain amount of yourself in it. There has to be, otherwise it's just not acting. It's lying."*   *Johnny Depp*

RE-CREATION AND INTERPRETATION

Playwrights, songwriters, and poets use their own lives as a resource for inspiration. Therefore, it can be useful to understand what kind of life or actual event may have inspired a song or literary work. The beauty of the performing arts, however, is that the lives of the creator and the re-creator converge in the performance. All human beings experience the same emotions, but there are unlimited variables when it comes to expressing them. Although it's helpful to learn through imitation, there comes a point where you must make your own choices and supply your own interpretation. This means using your own life and the lives of others, and combining them with the background and theatrical work of the composer/lyricist and playwright.

> *"All things have been given to us for a purpose, and an artist must feel this more intensely. All that happens to us, including our humiliations, our misfortunes, our embarrassments, all is given to us as raw material, as clay, so that we may shape our art."*   *Jorge Luis Borges*

WHAT IS ART?

The philosopher, Susanne Langer, best described "art" when she provided the following definition: "Art is the creation of forms symbolic of human feeling." Therefore, understanding feeling, your own feelings and those of others, is at the heart of being a singing actor. By expressing these feelings in "symbolic forms" (the music and text of opera, musical theatre, jazz, pop, rap, etc.), you can elevate that feeling into something that goes beyond explanation. Singing is elevated and sustained speech that probably grew from great emotion--the wail of grief, the whoop of a successful hunt, and the awe of the spiritual unknown. That's why, in a musical, the singing occurs when the words are no longer enough. The song is the culmination of what has happened before, not an interruption in the action.

Note: Don't let SUBSTITUTION get too complicated. If you're trying to substitute ten years of experiences and images in one song, you may simply have too many layers to navigate. You may end up looking strained and confused. Sometimes it's okay to simply pretend as you explore the WHAT IF of the situation. The game of pretend was once something you did naturally when passing cars would turn into dragons, a pile of rocks would become the walls of your castle, or your swing set would become a pirate ship. Think of acting as a wonderful excuse to play make believe.

SUBSTITUTION – Practice Repertoire/Exercises

Use the repertoire in the proceeding chapters and SUBSTITUTE your own life experiences for those of the characters. Practice a particular song as if *you* are the leading character and the story is your own. For example, "You Can't Stop the Beat" from *Hairspray* could reflect how you feel about getting into the college of your choice or landing a job you've always wanted. "What a Wonderful World" might be the response to your own house during the holidays. "Defying Gravity" from *Wicked* might reflect your determination to audition and win a coveted role.

Chapter 7

SUBTEXT AND PARAPHRASING

What are you really saying?

SUBTEXT IN THE MUSIC

Formal acting classes will often approach IMAGERY, SENSE MEMORY, SUBSTITUTION, and other elements of theatre in an organic way through a long process of discovery. This, of course, is valuable for any actor, but the singer has the added constraints of the music, and this may mean he or she must make more immediate and specific choices. Despite these limitations, there are also benefits. The singer has the visceral, non-verbal elements of music to draw on--a powerful beat that drives one to madness, a sweet melody that underscores a loving touch, or an agonizing chord stream that supplements a downstage cross to a dying lover. The music has a nonverbal power that can express the raw feeling of the words they support. For the singer, the music provides the words with a SUBTEXT, the feeling behind the words. In fact, it's not just the music that accompanies the singing voice that is revealing. The instrumental music that underscores the action and the dialogue also provides an emotional context that informs your acting choices.

> **"An ounce of behavior is worth a pound of words."**
> **Sanford Meisner**

SUBTEXT IN THE WORDS

For the non-singing actor, SUBTEXT is thought of in a slightly different way. It refers to the *real* meaning behind the words, the meaning that is expressed through inflection and body language. To put it simply, how we say something is far more revealing that what we say. If you want to be an effective performer that moves an audience, you must understand and utilize this SUBTEXT.

While the text often supplies your audience with *intellectual* information, your body language and vocal inflection supply the audience with *emotional* information. Usually the SUBTEXT reflects the text, even though it may supply it with more or less intensity. Sometimes, however, the SUBTEXT may even contradict the text. If someone says "I'd like for you to come to my party" with a warm smile and a gentle gesture, you will probably be happy to be invited in such a pleasant way. If, however, the same line is delivered with rolled eyes, folded arms, and a voice dripping with sarcasm and disdain, you can safely assume that the invitation is anything *but* sincere.

Even a slight change in word emphasis can reveal a new subtext. If the word, "you" is emphasized ("I'd like for *you* to come to my party."), the person inviting you has made it clear that the party won't be the same without "you." A good lyricist and composer will know how to use the strong and weak beats of the music to clarify the meaning in the words, and a good composer will know how to enhance the words and SUBTEXT in the accompaniment.

SUBTEXT AND THE SINGER

For the singer, since the SUBTEXT and the music go hand in hand, the entire piece of music must be studied as a whole.

The melody line in Stephen Sondheim's "Getting Married Today" is fairly mundane, but when his brilliant lyrics are coupled with the frantic musical accompaniment, the fear of marriage is palpable. This is a good example of why a singer must be careful when using a lead-sheet at an audition. The lead-sheet leaves out everything but the melody and the chord changes, so the accompaniment is left up to the pianist. The pianist may or may not know the details in the actual accompaniment that reflect the mood and intent of the piece. Granted, in some periods of music, the accompaniment is secondary, but for composers like Jason Robert Brown or Leonard Bernstein, the piano accompaniment and/or orchestrations are vital to the subtext, mood, and intensity of their works. Certainly, a dark foreboding legato cello in the accompaniment is quite a dramatic contrast to a perky, upper-register flute or clarinet.

The composer may sometimes provide a contradictory SUBTEXT in the accompaniment. A trite little song with nursery rhyme lyrics that is accompanied by a disturbing atonal dissonance can take the song from endearing to creepy. Film composers know how effective this is when they underscore the action of a happy little picnic with a foreboding melody, emotionally informing us that something bad is about to happen.

PARAPHRASING

PARAPHRASING is one of the best devices for understanding SUBTEXT and creating an honest performance. This is because, by putting the text and/or lyrics into your own words, you will find a personal connection to the material. If you PARAPHRASE, phrase by phrase, you will not only better understand the text; you will also understand how one idea flows into another. This can't help but provide you with more honest gestures and facial expressions, especially when you are dealing with the poetry of lyrics.

For example:

LYRIC: "I will reach through the stars to hold you close to my heart."

PARAPHRASE: (Using imagery and a personal WHOM substitution) "I will hold my arms out to you until you touch my hand, and then I will pull you close until you are cradled in my arms."

This especially helps when the subtext contradicts the text.

LYRIC: "You better not come around here anymore."

PARAPHRASE WITH CONTRADICTORY SUBTEXT: (Said with a smile and a wink) "Maybe if I tease and play a little hard to get, you'll be tempted to come see me again."

Certainly you have to consider the context of the song in the script, along with the wants and needs of the character, in order to understand and express the SUBTEXT. On the other hand, sometimes filling out the SUBTEXT helps you discover the character's wants and needs (as well as the WHOM and WHERE).

LYRIC: "I like the way you look at me but you may not see tomorrow."

PARAPHRASE: (filled out with IMAGERY and SENSE MEMORY) "Billy Flinchum, I just love the way you throw rocks at my window in the middle of the night, but I'm scared my Pa will find out. Nobody's good enough for his little girl, and he just happens to have a gun. I'd hate to see you get shot before we have our first kiss."

> *"Acting doesn't have anything to do with listening to the words. We never really listen, in general conversation, to what the other person is saying. We listen to what they mean. And what they mean is often quite apart from the words. When you see a scene between two actors that goes really well you can be sure they're not listening to each other. They're feeling what the other person is trying to get at."*   *Jack Lemmon*

POETIC LYRICS AND SUBTEXT

SUBTEXT can be a special challenge for singers since so many song lyrics are written in broad poetic metaphors that lack specific references. "My heart is soaring, our love is true," is a vague lyric that, without specific imagery, can result in a phony lovesick gaze. Therefore, you must decide what the lyrics mean. You must give them context and make sense out of them.

The best way to fill out your specific SUBTEXT is to PARAPHRASE the lyrics. Again, by putting the lyrics into your own words and filling them out with details, you will better understand the significance of the words. You can also fill out your imagery as you do this. For example, you could PARAPHRASE the lyrics *"My heart is soaring, our love is true"* into a more natural, *"I'm so happy you just said 'yes' to me here in the very place we first met. I can hardly catch my breath as you stand there smiling at me."* Once you put the text in your own words, you should then speak or sing the original text. This time, however, it should be imbued with the sincere body language, inflection, and imagery of the PARAPHRASED version.

109

When you must sing something from another era, such as the maudlin, 19th Century love song below, the period lyrics can be a challenge. This is also true for many period opera arias and art songs that have poetic lyrics that are more relevant to the period they were composed in. When you PARAPHRASE these period lyrics into a text you can personally relate to, your SUBTEXT will become clear and your delivery will be more honest.

For example:

LYRIC:

I love thee. I love thee.

Tis all that I can say.

It is the beating of my heart

My solace in the day

LINE BY LINE PARAPHRASE:

(Fill in a specific WHOM, WHERE, WHEN, and add the circumstances before you PARAPHRASE, especially if the song isn't part of a script.)

(**I love thee**) This is the first time I've told you this, so I hope that you'll listen carefully.

(**I love thee**) Please don't walk away from me. I have something you must hear.

Notice the change in SUBTEXT on the repeated line. Just because it is the same line, it doesn't mean that it must

have the same SUBTEXT. The second SUBTEXT might even cause you to reach out to your WHOM in a natural way.

(Tis all that I can say.) It's not enough, but it's the only way I know to express how I feel.

(It is the beating of my heart) Last night I sat in my dark bedroom, thinking of you. All I could hear was my own heart beat.

(My solace in the day) When I woke up this morning, I had a special feeling, and now that you are smiling at me, I know that everything will be okay.

NOTE: As a singer, you can use a metaphor in a somewhat literal sense to physically express a heightened emotion. If you say "Curtain up" as a way of expressing a new beginning in your life, you can gesture in an almost literal way. If you "raise that curtain" and see the lights and audience, your SUBSTITUTION will still elicit the "real" emotion of new possibilities. If you must "reach out" to the heavens to rescue you from your torment in an opera aria, you may actually extend your arms as if you are reaching for a rescue helicopter.

EXERCISES

1. *Decide on a word that has an emotional context. (For example: "reluctant, frightened, overjoyed, or suspicious.") After deciding on a WHOM, a WHERE, and a WHEN, as well as a set of circumstances, say the word over and over, but as you do, change your SUBTEXT and imagery. Keep a running monologue in your head as you act out the scene, a scene that should include a few twists and turns. For example, if you use the word "love" provide a SUBTEXT that moves from explaining the happiness of a new relationship to sharing the worry that you may be jumping into the relationship too soon (all the while repeating the word "love"). Your body language and vocal inflection will change as your SUBTEXT and imagery changes.*

    For example:

    The word is "savor"

    As you repeat the word, place yourself in front of a glass counter filled with delicious chocolates (WHERE). "Ask" the clerk (a WHOM) how many calories there are in the mouth-watering chocolate caramel almond delights. (This is an inner dialogue since you are only repeating the word "savor.") After she tells you that the calories equal more than a meal, you hesitate, struggling with your conflict between the taste and your diet. You start to walk out, but, as you do, you notice a child biting into one of the scrumptious delights. You return to the clerk (while still repeating the word "savor") and ask if there is anything with fewer calories. You take a minute to decide if a tiny, low-calorie wafer will satisfy you. Reluctantly, you take it, but as you turn, you see the child, smiling as she takes the last bite. You rush back to the counter and order the chocolate. (And the entire time all you have said is the word, "savor.")

2. Pick a song that you have memorized. After deciding on your images and a general subtext, "sing" the song without using your voice. Instead create a "ts" sound that pushes back on the release of air with your teeth, allowing you to feel the connection to your diaphragm. "Sing" the song with this sound as you fill out the inner monologue, the SUBTEXT. Even though you are not using words, you will still have a sense of the phrasing because of the breath. Let the air soar as the music and subtext soars.

3. Pick a situation, two characters, and a WHERE. With a friend, proceed to have a conversation. However, the only words you are allowed to say are "peanut butter."

For example:

You both are spies who are ready to break into the headquarters of the enemy to steal a secret code. You must plan the final strategy now that you've seen the entrance to the headquarters, but you disagree on the best way to break in. There are guards everywhere and there are sweeping lights that nearly give away your hiding place. You must come to an agreement quickly.

Your body language, vocal color, and vocal inflection will bring about a surprisingly complete conversation. Remember, don't use charade-like gestures to make a point. (Although you may find yourself using a gesture that involves looking at and tapping your watch to point out that time is of the essence. Just don't tap on your watch to get someone to guess you are talking about time.)

4. *Pretend you are giving "how to" instructions to an audience. Again, you are only allowed to use the words, "peanut butter." Don't mime the props. Simply provide a verbal explanation that may, from time to time, include natural gestures that refer to your props ("Find a bowl about this big."). Keep your audience active by making them confused, excited, unruly, etc.*

For example:

Audience: *Immigrants who can't speak English.*

Topic: *How to fill out a citizenship application.*

(Okay, this one may require a few "indicating" gestures.)

Audience: *Senior citizens with no computer experience.*

Topic: *How to build a Facebook page.*

Audience: *A group of excited fourth graders.*

Topic: *Their first lesson on how to play the saxophone.*

Audience: *Basketball team*

Topic: *Explaining strategies for the next game.*

5. *Try paraphrasing these tacky lyrics. Challenge yourself to include the circumstances and the sensory details of the WHOM, WHERE, and WHEN as you paraphrase.*

   For example:

   Lyric: *"You light the candle that glows within me."*

   Translation: *"With you in my life, I don't sleep through the alarm anymore. I can't wait for a new day, shopping for our dinner and buying funny greeting cards to share with you. I even enjoy going to work because everyone there asks about you. To the core, I am happy."*

   Use these lyric examples or make up your own:

   "Your heart is cold."

   "Why walk when we can fly?"

   "The heartache is over, but my life is too."

   "Why, God, why me?"

   "Behold, love's arrow has left its idle bow."

6. *Select a ballad from your repertoire that isn't from a musical. Select a WHOM, a WHERE, and a WHEN. Also, remember to create a "moment before"--the reason you are singing this song. Before you sing, PARAPHRASE the lyrics so that they include the SUBTEXT, the real meaning behind the words. If you have a recording of the music, speak the SUBTEXT/PARAPHRASE while the music is playing to set the mood. Then, sing the song as you maintain the emotional integrity you discovered in the PARAPHRASED version.*

7. *Repeat Exercise #7, but this time use an up-tempo from your repertoire.*

8. *Shake it up. Try something with a ridiculous line of action such as an alien invasion (ala <u>Little Shop of Horrors</u>). You are the only one who speaks their language, and you must talk them out of destroying the earth. Sing your argument in the alien's language—an alien opera aria of sorts. The words will obviously be nonsense, but the meaning should still be clear. Try other absurd situations and scenarios to challenge your imagination.*

9. *Have a friend speak to "an audience" in the nonsense language of Slavaconian. You will serve as the translator for his or her lecture. Using your friend's body language and inflection as clues, interpret the lecture for the non-Slavaconian-speaking audience.*

SUBTEXT and PARAPHRASE – Practice Repertoire

Utilizing the repertoire from the preceding chapters, PARAPHRASE a song using two contrasting SUBTEXTS.

FINAL THOUGHTS ON PART I

> *"It would be possible to describe everything scientifically, but it would make no sense; it would be without meaning, as if you described a Beethoven symphony as a variation of wave pressure."*
>   *Albert Einstein*

THAT'S ONLY HALF OF THE STORY

You have lots of paint on your palate at this point, but you're far from done. Now you must learn how to use that "paint" to create a work of art. It's time to study, as Susanne Langer puts it, the "FORM symbolic of human feeling." In Part II, you will do just that as you learn to apply the Part I principles to artistic FORM. This learning process isn't a calculation or a formula. It is a trial-and-error process based on the principles of human feeling. It can lead to the "aha" and "wow" moments most artists live for, and despite some frustrations and failures, it is well worth the effort.

PART II

THE WINE AND THE BOTTLE

Feeling and Form

AN OVERVIEW

A great singer is not necessarily a great performer, especially if he or she doesn't understand how to physically present a song. A great "emoter" is not necessarily a great actor, especially if he or she doesn't understand that acting is an art form. Besides using your imagination to create a vivid sensory life, you will also need to understand the relationship between the ingredients of emotion (accessed through IMAGERY and SENSE MEMORY) and the elements of form (the organization and presentation of these emotional ingredients).

As a singer, you must be more than a conduit for tonal resonance and vocal acrobatics. As an actor, you must be more than a conduit for tears and laughter. If you truly want to be an artist, these technical and emotional feats must work in tandem with the elements of form to create an artistic whole.

In order for an artist to perform with integrity, there must be a balance between feeling and form. Think of the feeling as THE WINE and the form as THE BOTTLE. THE WINE, the "feeling," is the raw physical and emotional expression of the voice and body. THE BOTTLE represents the elements of form that hold these the emotional elements together. When the two are successfully combined, there is a common ground for artistic expression. When the form and feeling of music and theatre converge, we have something especially magical.

> *"I regard the theatre as the greatest of all art forms, the most immediate way in which a human being can share with another the sense of what it is to be a human being."*
> *Oscar Wilde*

Chapter 8

THE WINE

The Flow of Feeling

You've already learned that IMAGERY and SENSE MEMORY are great ways to access and respond to emotion. When you are engaged in this recollection (or make-believe), you respond with an intuitive emotional energy. For this to happen, however, it is often necessary to learn how to quiet the analytical side of your brain and shut down the social inhibitors you've acquired through years of socialization. That means you must develop a healthy dose of "letting go" to develop your imagination. (Remember that "fun" is *not* a dirty word! "Fun" shuts down inhibitors to ideas.)

> *"The creation of something new is not accomplished by the intellect, but by the play instinct acting from inner necessity. The creative mind plays with the objects it loves."*   *Carl Gustav Jung*

The following exercises are designed to shut down those social inhibitors and beef up your imagination and intuition.

1. *Change your routine. Don't wear make-up if you usually do. Wear make-up if you don't. Wear something you wouldn't normally wear. Sit in a different seat each time you go to class, or take a different route to work. Skip*

instead of walk, do a pirouette in the grocery store aisle, or enjoy a children's game. This may all may sound blasphemous to the mature adult, but that safe and dependable box you've grown accustomed to can be stale and repetitive.

Note: Change activates the senses. For example, think of how alive you feel when the seasons change. Change can also be uncomfortable, but that discomfort also activates the senses. Give yourself permission to step outside of the box, even if it is a little scary.

---

2. *Creativity is a messy process, so let yourself be messy! Splash through mud puddles in the pouring rain. Let melting ice cream drip all over your shirt. Make snow angels and throw snowballs. Rip pages out of an old phone book or magazine, and throw them around the house. Fingerpaint all over the page or the wall. Squeeze clay through your fingers without making forms.*

3. *Liberate yourself from social restrictions (legally, of course.). Shout until you can hear your echo between two buildings. Sing old camp songs in the shower. Jump rope singing out playground chants (cardio at the gym doesn't count.) Treat yourself to a game of laser tag, or better yet, a game of paint ball.*

4. *Gather a wide variety of music, giving special attention to styles and genres you don't normally listen to. Then, close the doors and windows, and while no one is looking, crank up the sound. March around the room to the beat; freely dance around the house; bounce on the bed. Using the music as inspiration, pretend you're a rock star, a country legend, a famous athlete, or a world class spy from a James Bond movie. Let the music wash over you as you respond*

to the beat, the soaring melody, the lyrics, or even the decibel level. LET YOURSELF GO!

The list of "letting go" exercises is endless, or at least it used to be before you forgot how to have fun, act silly, and laugh until your side ached.

Note: Remember, alcohol isn't allowed. That would be cheating. In fact, maybe the reason people drink is to have an excuse to act a little crazy. "Well, I was drunk." Wouldn't it be great if we could just "be free" without an excuse or a reason?

CREATIVITY AND CHOICE

The foundation of any art form is CREATIVITY, and the foundation of creativity is CHOICE. Most of your school years will be focused on acquiring and memorizing the right answers to a multitude of questions. As an artist, however, (and you can't be reminded enough) you must learn to continually search for the strongest choice. Of course, this choice will have limitations when it comes to style, period, medium, genre, and dramatic context, and you will also have to consider your audience and your own technical limitations. Nonetheless, you will still be seeking the strongest choice. There will be endless variables that will keep you on your toes. The actor you are sharing a scene with may deliver lines in a way you don't expect; a fortissimo might not be technically possible for you; the director may have something else in mind; or the audience may not find your choice particularly moving. That's why you must be willing to bob-and-weave during this process. Sometimes you'll even find that your initial choice was the best one, but how will you know it's the best choice unless you've tried out the weaker ones. Sometimes you'll simply need to arrive at new choices to keep yourself fresh as a performer. After a year-long run, grieving the loss of your lover the same way every night can get old.

Note: You may find yourself making great choices that never even occurred to your teacher. A good teacher won't be threatened by this, but will revel in the fact that you've jumped into the deep end of ideas. A *great* teacher will then give guidance as to the best way to navigate those ideas.

"A teacher is never a giver of truth. He's a guide, a pointer to the truth that each student must find for himself."
                                                                        Bruce Lee

EXERCISES

The following exercises also include some group exercises, so gather your friends and family for some fun!

1. *Play games that involve physical and verbal communication, such as Charades and Password. You can even pass a story around the room, with one person supplying a few sentences, and the next one adding more to the tale. (That way, you can't plan and will stay in the moment.) Allow yourself to visualize the story as it progresses, filling in sensory details in your mind. This will also help you be a more descriptive storyteller.*

2. *Write down random words on individual pieces of paper (words like "heart," "car," "chair," "jealous," etc.) Put the words in a hat and divide into two teams. The first player on Team A will draw one of the words and, within a minute, must sing at least 8 words of a musical phrase that uses that word (from a recognizable song). If there is still*

time remaining, the next person on Team A will do the same thing until the time is up for that team. Team B will then repeat the same process. When all of the words are gone from the hat, each team counts up the words they've successfully put to music.

3. *Watch "Whose Line is it Anyway" or buy a book of theatrical improvisation games. These games are not only fun, but are a great way to speed up your creative thinking and expressive responses. During improvisation games, when someone "throws" the metaphorical ball, you have to watch and listen in order to "catch it" and "throw it back."*

> **Note: If you feel that your choices, answers, and creative responses aren't very good, don't worry about it. If you are constantly judging your performance during the creative process, you will never let go enough to enjoy the freedom of what is often referred to as "creative flow", the stream of ideas that occur without effort. Who knows? Maybe what may initially seem like a "bad" idea will turn out to be a good one. Artists call these "happy accidents."**

4. *Play instrumental music that is not associated with a storyline. Close your eyes and imagine what action it would underscore if you were making a movie. Put yourself into the story and include lots of sensory details.*

5. *Play a game of alphabet improvisation using your own biography—something about you or your family, or something that happened during your day. Pick a letter from the alphabet, and provide a line that starts with that letter for a monologue. Continue until you've gone the full circle of the alphabet. (For "x", use any words that begin with "ex" like "excellent" or "extraordinary.")*

For example: (To your best friend)

J - *Jerry hasn't called me all day.*

K – *Know why? 'Cause it's all about Susan.*

L - *Like Susan could actually make him happier than me.*

M - *Maybe if I could just tell him how I feel...*

N – *No way. He's gonna have to say it first.*

O - *Oh, for goodness sake, stop looking at me like that.*

P – *Please, just stop judging me.*

Continue until you've made it once around the alphabet.

This time, let the alphabetical phrases follow a WHERE.

C - *Colorado mountains on a cool spring day make me happy.*

D - *Deer are grazing in front of me.*

E - *Every once in awhile, they look up when they hear me rustling the bushes.*

F - *Forests are so peaceful.*

You can also try this exercise as a dialogue, alternating each line with a scene partner.

Character 1: *Teaching children is not my forte.*

Character 2: *Unfortunately for you, you're a teacher.*

Character 1: *Very nice of you to remind me on the worst day of my life.*

Character 2: *Why don't you do something else for a living?*

Character 1: *Excellent idea.*

Character 2: *You're welcome.*

Chapter 9

THE BOTTLE

The Form of Feeling

Artistic form, THE BOTTLE, does for feeling what reading and writing do for thinking. Just as reading and writing allow us to express and share our intellectual experiences, artistic forms allow us to express and share the experience of human feeling.

> *"Emotional release by itself, no matter how real or honest the emotion may be, is never enough to create a character...such release has no artistic form."*
> **Richard Hornby**

It's difficult to separate FEELING AND FORM because one is so dependent on the other. It isn't as simple as putting the FEELING into FORM because feeling *itself* has form. As human beings, we respond to this emotional structure. For example, if the curtain opens and you, as an audience member, see a character on stage crying without any context, you will conceptually recognize the fact that *someone is sad*. If, however, the curtain opens and over the course of the musical or play (or even over the course of a song), you see this character struggle to maintain her happiness and her dignity until she is ultimately brought to her knees in despair, you will have observed and responded to emotional form. Instead of intellectually labeling a human emotion, you will be invested in the journey of human emotion.

> *All things have been given to us for a purpose and an artist must feel this more intensely. All that happens to us, including our humiliations, our misfortunes, our embarrassments, all is given to us as raw material, as clay, so that we may shape our art."* **Jorge Luis Borges**

You might be even more engaged if, in earlier scenes, you had witnessed the happiness this character once knew. You might even experience her plight more intensely if her emotional journey is musically underscored or expressed with poetic lyrics. When choices are made that effectively bring all of these elements together, you, as an audience member, will not only *sympathize* with the character, you will *empathize* with her as well—you will identify with her feelings. Even though you may not share her history or her point of view, you will have shared the power of her emotional experience. You are no longer a bystander.

> **NOTE: The audience doesn't want to see your technique when you are sharing an emotional experience. A dropped jaw is helpful for your vocal technique, but if you lose all expression because of it, you have compromised your performance.**

> *"Every little moment has a meaning all its own."*
> *Karl Hoschna*

THE BEGINNING, MIDDLE, AND END

Since theatre and music are art forms that exist in time, it stands to reason that they will have a beginning, a middle, and an end. For the actor and the singer, however, the beginning, the middle, and the end must be made up of smaller moments that flow one into the next. The moments eventually come together to form a bigger picture. In acting, these moments are often referred to as BEATS (whereas the word for the singer refers to a basic unit of time, a pulse). More often, however, the acting term, BEAT, refers to the pauses, the moments of silence, between the action when the actor changes the mood, the intent, or the objective. The moment-to-moment BEATS *and* the pause-in-the-action BEATS are usually dripping with subtext, and they will eventually come together in a way that will give a song an expressive form.

> *"When actors are talking, they are servants of the dramatist; it is what they can show the audience when they are not talking that reveals the fine actor."*
> *Cedric Hardwicke*

NOTE: Remember, we see something before we respond to it. We savor the look of the chocolate before we reach for it; we squint at the shadowy figure before we gasp, and we gasp before we run away from it. This is the moment-to-moment business of acting.

In a song, these transitional pauses, these BEATS, are often accompanied by a rest or a cadence. Instead of using these moments to clear your throat, re-set your posture, or seat your breath, you must keep these "in between" moments theatrically alive. Instead of regrouping, this is when you see, feel, or hear something that motivates you to express the next moment.

Think about the individual "beats" that occur throughout your day. For example, a typical morning might have a number of transitional moments.

(The sound of the alarm)

Huh? What the...(BEAT)

Oh, the alarm. Oh, well, I'll just catch a few more z's.

And these covers are so warm and...(BEAT)

Oh, that yapping dog across the street...(BEAT)

Oh, well. I'll talk to the neighbors about him later. Just a few more minutes...(BEAT)

Oh, no, wait... what time is it?

6:00?... (BEAT)

Oh, no. I have an audition at 8:00.

Well, maybe I have time for just a couple more...(BEAT)

Oh, no, I can't. I didn't get the directions last night...(BEAT)

I'm up. I'm up...(BEAT)

And I'm thirsty.

(A glance in the mirror) (BEAT)

I should've got a haircut. (BEAT)

But who can afford a haircut without a job?

It's the moments of transition that are loaded with feeling and emotional information. Some beats are longer than others, but the most important thing is to honor them, in a scene or a song.

"The play is not in the words. It's in you!"
                                    Stella Adler

EXERCISES

1. *Imagine a short scene from your day. Go through the beat-by-beat action in your mind. Then, take three "photographs" of the scene by freezing in tableau. The first tableau "photo" should be at the beginning of your scene. The second should take place in the middle and should reflect a transition of some kind. The last tableau "photograph" should be taken at the end of your scene. Remind yourself of the action that occurred between the "photographs" (the tableaus).*

2. *Make up a dozen unrelated sentences. Put them in a hat, and draw three of these random phrases. For example, you may end up with something like this:*

   "Janet came over last night without any warning."
   "I've always loved the tango."
   "I just won't eat onions anymore."

135

Let each phrase provide you with a beginning, a middle, and an end for a short monologue. Choose a WHOM and then connect each phrase with consecutive BEATS.

For example:

"Janet came over last night without any warning."

"At first, I was angry that she showed up, especially after that disastrous date we had at the reunion. Remember? All she did was drink, and she wouldn't dance with me, not once. Then, I realized, when I saw her face last night, that she felt bad about it. She smiled and then handed me a class schedule for dance lessons and said..."

"I've always loved the tango."

"She had signed us up for dance classes. And then, she took my hand and said, 'To make up for the other night, I've made reservations at that Brazilian restaurant you've always liked.' I wanted to play a little hard to get. Right? I mean, I want to keep her on her toes, so she doesn't take me for granted again, so I said, "Okay, I'll go dancing, but I'm not interested in the Brazilian food. It's too spicy and loaded with onions, and..."

"I just don't eat onions anymore."

NOTE: Singers often have to "fill in" the acting moments during musical interludes. It's important to connect the acting beats from the last phrase before the interlude to the first phrase after it in order to maintain the emotional momentum.

---

3. *Be aware of your inner monologue while doing a mundane task, such as making the beds, washing the car, or putting*

your groceries away after shopping. Verbalize your thought process and the feelings that occur from moment to moment while performing this task. Take special note of the transitional BEATS that occur.

For example: (... = transitional BEATS)

"I hope the canned goods aren't scattered all over the trunk. It sure sounded like it when I turned the corner... Damn, the lock is so hot. I'm sick of this crazy weather... Okay, everything looks pretty good... Gosh, do I want to carry this stuff in all at once? The bags will probably break if I try that... I sure wish Scott was here to help me out. He would have politely carried the whole shopping in if I hadn't been so mean to him this morning... Oh, well, I'll have to remember to be on my best behavior next time I'm thinking about going shopping...Oh, no where's the dog food?... Oh great! I left the stupid dog food in the bottom of the cart."

4. *Select a song, preferably a musical theatre selection or an opera aria. Mark the transitional BEATS in the music. (You may want to establish a SUBTEXT first to help you interpret the lyrics.) Don't forget that these BEATS occur during the instrumental introduction and interludes as well as the sung phrases.*

Chapter 10

THE BEFORE/THE BACKSTORY

"How did we end up here?"

THE BEFORE-THE BACKSTORY-THE BEGINNING

In order to have a strong beginning, you must first choose what has happened before you sing your first note or speak your first word. This BEFORE is also referred to as the BACKSTORY. The BACKSTORY can go back years ("After all this time, why are you telling me you love me now?") or it can be only moments old ("Who are you, and why are you following me?") THE MOMENT BEFORE is a springboard for the first words of your song or monologue. If your initial lyrics are "I hate you!" at a fortissimo, it will be important to know what has just happened to elicit this response.

For singers, the MOMENT BEFORE usually occurs in the musical introduction. Thus, the acting actually starts with the first note of the accompaniment, not the first word out of your mouth. Unfortunately, many singers use the musical introduction as a time to adjust their clothing, fix their hair, and clear their throat instead of engaging in their image. When the singer suddenly engages on the first sung note, it creates a sort of dramatic whiplash.

> **NOTE: Even a simple bell tone can provide a MOMENT BEFORE.** One note can signify an "aha," a sudden idea, a moment of surprise, or a flirtatious "wink." If you have a bell tone or a very short introduction for an audition, use it to set up your first words. In fact, regardless of the length, use the introduction for the MOMENT BEFORE. Don't use it to stare at your accompanist, unless your accompanist is your image!

INTERNALIZING A BEFORE

Besides being engaged in your IMAGERY during the musical introduction or interlude, it's sometimes helpful to use an internal monologue to propel you into the song.

Internal MOMENT BEFORE: *(To your WHOM)*
> "Don't cry. It'll be okay."

Opening lyric:
> "Smile though your heart is breaking."

Internal MOMENT BEFORE: (*Responding to your WHERE***)**
> "How will I ever get this packing done? Every
> item holds so many memories."

Opening lyric:
> "Where do you start? How do you separate the
> present from the past."

Internal MOMENT BEFORE: *(Your WHOM speaking to you.)*
> "But I don't want to go to bed, Mom."

Opening lyric:
> "If you go to sleep, sweet dreams await you."

You can also imagine how changing the internal "before moment" might change the delivery of the first spoken or sung line:

Internal MOMENT BEFORE:
> "What a wonderful surprise birthday party. You're the best!

Opening lyric:
> "I can't imagine living life without you."

As opposed to:

Internal MOMENT BEFORE:
> "Please be safe on the battleground tonight."

Opening lyric:
> "I can't imagine living life without you."

BREATH AND THE BEFORE

You not only express your feelings through your body and voice as you exhale on the tone; you also express yourself when you inhale. A gasp might precede "Oh no, he's here!" or the inhale of a sigh might be followed by "I wish she loved me that way." The MOMENT BEFORE includes the inhale, and your inhale affects how you exhale, which in turn affects your vocal and physical delivery. Long, drawn out nasal breaths are terrific for your vocal technique, but if all of your breaths are alike, you will be asking your audience to suspend the fantasy every time you inhale. No one wants to watch your breathing technique. Your breathing technique is there to serve a greater purpose.

> **NOTE: Even visceral responses, such as a scream or an outburst of laughter, have moments before. It may be the quiet, dark silence that precedes a scream or the smirk on your friend's face that sends you over the edge with laughter.**

POLISHING YOUR BACKSTORY

It's important to understand the LONGTERM BACKSTORY for a song in order to understand its context and intent. A RECENT BACKSTORY simply adds more relevant details to the LONGTERM BACKSTORY. THE MOMENT BEFORE is the beat or two that occurs just before you sing—the acting BEAT that propels you into the song.

Examples of LONGTERM, RECENT, and MOMENT BEFORE BACKSTORIES:

> **LONGTERM BACKSTORY**: "I've wanted a meaningful relationship for a long time."

> **A RECENT BACKSTORY**: "There's this girl in my history class. The first time I saw her she ignored me, but lately we've been having some great conversations. She likes it when I tell how pretty she looks. I'm considering asking her for coffee after class. Who knows? Maybe she's the one."

> **THE MOMENT BEFORE**: "She's smiling at me and motioning for me to join her. She actually saved a seat for me! She looks like she's so happy to see me. Well, here goes."

> **OPENING LYRIC**: "Hey good lookin', what ya got cookin? How's about cookin' somethin' up with me?"

NOTE: As human beings, we simply respond more authentically to specific moments than broad concepts. You may know about the ASPCA and feel bad that some animals must be put down, but you may not have the money to support the organization. However, the minute you see a commercial with the sweet face of a wide-eyed puppy or kitten, your emotional responses overtake your intellectual ones, and you're suddenly digging through your pockets for change. Add musical underscore (the SUBTEXT) to the commercial, and you're taking out a loan at the bank.

EXERCISES

1. In the following exercise, the LONGTERM BACKSTORY and the opening lyrics are provided. Fill in the specifics for the RECENT BACKSTORY and the MOMENT BEFORE inner monologues that might occur during a musical introduction. For example:

    LONGTERM BACKSTORY: "You've never treated me with love and respect."
    RECENT BACKSTORY: "Why do I still care about you after the way you cheated on me?"
    MOMENT BEFORE: "I must be out of my mind."
    OPENING LYRIC: "Why do I always come back to you?"

LONGTERM: "I've always wanted to be a star."
RECENT:_____
MOMENT BEFORE:_____
OPENING LYRIC: "I'm going to make it this time."

LONGTERM: *"We can do anything if we're together."*
RECENT:_____
MOMENT BEFORE:_____
OPENING LYRIC: *"We can take on the world."*

LONGTERM: *"One day, things will be different."*
RECENT:_____
MOMENT BEFORE:_____
OPENING LYRIC: *"Let's get away from here."*

2. *Create a BROAD BACKSTORY, a RECENT (detailed) BACKSTORY, and a MOMENT BEFORE for an actual song lyric. (See the Practice Repertoire lists included in previous chapters for ideas.) If it is a musical theatre or opera selection, try using the actual context of the piece within the storyline, or stretch your imagination by using a completely original BACKSTORY.*

3. *Choose a song and provide three contrasting BEFORE MOMENTS. Instead of internalizing them, say them out loud. Notice how the BEFORE changes the song.*

For example (Song: "My Favorite Things")

MOMENT BEFORE #1: *(The actual BEFORE) "Don't be afraid, children, because I can think of something that will make you feel better."*

MOMENT BEFORE #2: *"I just love this little gift shop...so many adorable little items. Take a look at all of the fun gifts we could buy the kids."*

MOMENT BEFORE #3: *"Listen, you little brats, we're not going to the toy store today. We're going to do what I want to do and buy what I want to buy."*

NOTE: In musical theatre, the MOMENT BEFORE is often in the form of underscored dialogue or an underscored monologue. It's important not to let the energy or the imagery drop in between the last spoken line and the first sung line. One moment should simply flow into the next.

BACKSTORY – Practice Repertoire

Utilizing the repertoire from the preceding chapters, either fill out the details for the existing BACKSTORY, or make up a new one.

Chapter 11

PROGRESSION/TRANSITION

The Ballet of Tension and Release

The audience may enjoy the PROGRESSION of a murder mystery as the playwright drops clue after clue that the butler has committed the murder. This, of course, builds the anticipation. However, there may a gradual TRANSITION when other clues suggest that the maid may be the guilty party. This creates even more anticipation and *tension*. At the climax, when the *tension* peaks, we find the detective sharing the mounting evidence. At this point, the playwright can either continue the anticipated PROGRESSION, or, perhaps, make a stronger choice with a sudden TRANSITION, indicating that there is yet another suspect. In the next moment, we discover that it is neither the butler nor the maid. It's the mistress of the house who has framed the poor servants! The mounting tension has been followed by a resolution that has released the suspense. Whatever the playwright's choices, the audience has observed and vicariously experienced an emotional PROGRESSION with various TRANSITIONS that create *tension* and *release* to heighten the collective experience. These are the elements of dramatic FORM.

THE MIDDLE – CREATING FORM

FORM isn't made up of some arbitrary set of rules handed down by the gods for each generation to obediently follow. FORM is, instead, a way of using the elements of our emotional lives in an organized way to evoke and share human feeling. We learn how to do this by studying and imitating artists who have successfully "moved" others with their art. Visual artists use such things as lighting contrasts and perspective to create FORM. Since theatre and music are art forms that move through time, composers and playwrights use elements that move through time to create FORM. By using PROGRESSION and TRANSITION, as well as repetition and contrast, musical and theatrical artists create a ballet of tension and release to evoke feeling. This tension and release occurs, not only in a theatrical or musical work, but in your everyday life as well.

> *"The human is indissolubly linked with imitation: a human being only becomes human at all by imitating other human beings."*   ***Theodor Adorno***

Just as the basics of human nature haven't changed throughout history, neither has the fundamental nature of art. The way we express ourselves, however, the way we frame feeling, changes constantly from generation to generation. Sometimes this expression changes profoundly from one person to another or even throughout the course of one person's day. This is why, as dramatic artists, we must be willing to adapt and change.

> *"There is no state of final fulfillment. Each change opens new doors and ushers in new possibilities."*
> ***Margo Adair***

At some point in history, a particular chord might have been considered dissonant, creating a disturbing tension. As people became accustomed to that chord, it probably began sounding consonant, even pleasing to the ear. An idea that was once blasphemous in one era ("What was that about the earth going around the sun?") may be perceived as common knowledge in the next generation. The sight of a woman's leg might have produced gasps in the Puritanical world of the early Americans, while today no one would give it a second thought.

Because of this, composers and playwrights must continually look for new ways to express old ideas. This is often met with opposition from the masses, but the artists forge on, knowing that art must change in order to remain relevant. The performing artist must also adapt to change--from style to style, role to role, and genre to genre. What's vital is to understand that the process, the technique, and the FORM are there to serve an internal life of feeling that can't be described in any other way.

> *"What is real is not the external form, but the essence of things... it is impossible for anyone to express anything essentially real by imitating its exterior surface."*
> *Constantin Brancusi*

CHANGE

Change activates the senses in a moment-to-moment way, whether it's the smell of the earth after the first spring rain or a new flavor of coffee at Starbucks. This change can be gradual, such as ascending higher and higher in a hot air balloon, or it can be sudden, as in the realization that you've won the lottery. Change makes us feel something, and we respond with goose bumps, or tears, or laughter. These reactions are a release, an expression, of what is within us. Without it, we can succumb to apathy and depression.

> *"We delight in the beauty of the butterfly but rarely admit the changes it has gone through to achieve that beauty."*
> *Maya Angelou*

PROGRESSION, TRANSITION, and RECAPITULATION

The repetitive part of a song may build by way of crescendos and modulations, creating a PROGRESSION. This activates something within us. We hang on for the ride, just as we hang on as the roller coaster ascends the track. This PROGRESSION builds until it is met with a contrasting moment. This TRANSITION elicits a contrasting feeling. (Just as the climbing roller coaster is followed by a "contrasting" plunge.)

After a TRANSITION, we may hunger for a return to the original theme, a "going home" if you will. Waiting for that return creates anticipation, and anticipation certainly creates feeling (ask any kid waiting for Santa Claus). That return becomes even more desirable if we have to wait for it a little longer than we expected. When we are finally handed what we've been waiting for, however, there is a release, an "ah" moment that creates yet another feeling in us. This return is something you will see in the ABA form in music. There is a theme, a departure, and a recap (recapitulation). This musical form is frequently used because it provides the repetition and contrast that creates the tension and release we like to experience as human beings.

PLAYING AGAINST THE ANGST

PROGRESSIONS and TRANSITIONS will also keep you from getting stuck in the "angst" (or "happy") of a song. Being able to cry and sob through a piece simply isn't the definition of acting. Although it's helpful to be able to access genuine feelings, that is only one component of your art form. If you fall into the Johnny-one-note trap, you won't be acknowledging the elements that give a work emotional texture and FORM. Your acting moments will flow one to the next without depth, without change.

Your audience will feel more empathy if they experience the complexity of human emotion, the good *and* the bad. If your character is suffering in despair, he or she may be fighting to find the joy again so as not to succumb to the pain. Even at the saddest funeral, there are those moments that evoke a happy memory. "Remember the time she had us all over for Thanksgiving and the oven broke? She ended up making us all scrambled eggs and bacon. It was the best Thanksgiving we ever had." That memory brings a smile to everyone's faces, making the next moment, the realization she's gone, even more poignant. Life is, indeed, a rich fabric of moment-to-moment emotion.

THE MUSIC **AND** THE ACTING

As an actor, your job is to create, respond to, and enhance the theatrical PROGRESSIONS and TRANSITIONS in a work. As an acting singer you must also reflect and respond to the musical PROGRESSIONS and TRANSITIONS. Your acting may have to adapt to the music more often than the other way around due to the constraints of time and the accompaniment, but the important thing to remember is that the acting and music must work in tandem. As a singing actor, you must listen closely to the music. Then, you must make acting choices accordingly. Does the musical bridge reflect a change in your IMAGERY, your mood, or your attitude? Does the musical climax release the emotion? Does a sweeping chord progression underscore an emotional progression? Is the diction more articulated with anger due to the dissonant syncopations in the accompaniment? Do your arms open up on the soaring phrases that reflect the love expressed in the lyrics? Does a sudden "railroad track" in the music provide you with a BEAT, a pause, to reconsider or reaffirm an acting moment? If you truly marry the acting and the music, your physical responses will be more than just a random set of accessories.

HOW ACTORS CREATE FORM

Musicians use harmonic, melodic, and rhythmic devices to create and enhance FORM. Actors use the responses to their WANTS and OBSTACLES by asking themselves the following questions:

What do I want?
What's in my way?
What will I do to get what I want?

Answering these questions, along with a strong sense of IMAGERY and a healthy dose of SENSE MEMORY, will ultimately help you integrate THE WINE and THE BOTTLE, and this will make all the difference in your performance.

> NOTE: Non-singing actors have more flexibility when it comes to timing dramatic pauses or actions. The singing actor, however, is often at the mercy of the tempos and pauses set by the conductor. Therefore, singing actors must be prepared and willing to adapt their acting to the music.

EXERCISES

1. *Beware aware of your daily responses to the elements of Progression, Transition, Repetition, Contrast, Anticipation, Tension and Release throughout your day. Not only recall how you felt when you experienced these elements, but also recall what you <u>did</u> when you felt a certain way.*

Progression: *If you are expecting an important phone call, feel the excitement build each time the phone rings. If you think you might be fired, feel how your nervous tension grows each time someone walks out of the boss' office with a dejected look. Feel the progression of energy in your office or classroom when bits and pieces of information contribute to a developing piece of gossip. (And note the anticipation as people grow hungry for more.)*

Anticipation: *Think about how anticipation heightens emotion, whether it's the anticipation of an answer to your proposal, a delicious dessert baking in the oven, or the hours before a blind date.*

Transition: *Does your significant other shock you when he or she does something entirely out of character? Perhaps your boyfriend remembers your birthday for the first time in five years, causing you to suddenly suspect something. Notice how the change of season, a change of flavor, or a change of routine affects you. Acknowledge the emotional difference between a sudden transition as opposed to a gradual one. For example, the difference between the loss of a game in sudden overtime as opposed to the gradual descent of your team from a winning streak to a series of defeats.*

Repetition and Contrast: *Study the parts of your day that are routine and uneventful. Then, recall the times that that routine has been upset with a fire alarm, an unexpected raise, or even a friendly smile from a usually somber receptionist. Does the contrasting event wake you up from you complacency? Does it heighten your awareness? Think about what you like and dislike about repetition and*

153

contrast. Are you bored with routine or uncomfortable with change?

Tension and Release: *Consider how all of the above circumstances create feeling. The butterflies of worry that give-way to the relief of "Oh, thank goodness." The stressful anticipation during labor followed by the relief that the baby is healthy. The "aha" moment after you've finally discovered the solution to a difficult problem. Remember, as an actor, be aware of both how you felt and how you acted.*

2. *Select a piece of instrumental music, preferably a colorful overture or a bold symphonic work. As you listen, decide where the music builds tension and where that tension is released. Determine the peaks in the music and analyze what devices the composer uses to build the climactic moments. Listen for transitions that change the mood or enhance the feeling in the music.*

3. *Take the same piece of music as in Exercise #2, but this time, create a story that goes with the music. Decide what action would best reflect the music, as if the selection was underscore for a movie storyline. Be specific by providing a WHOM, a WHERE, and moment-to-moment SENSE MEMORY.*

4. *Select various vocal works and study the text in relationship to the music. Notice how the music and lyrics do or don't work together to create feeling and form.*

5. *Select a song to sing with a variety of subtexts. Listen to the musical accompaniment for your initial choices, but then provide a contrasting subtext in order to play against*

the original one. If the song is happy, provide a more serious subtext and vice versa. Imagine how the musical accompaniment would change with a contrasting underscore.

For example: (Song: "Mary had a Little Lamb")

Obvious SUBTEXT: *Isn't that cute? Mary's little lamb loves her so much, it follows her to school every single day.*

Contrasting SUBTEXT: *This lamb is creating a problem for Mary. No matter what she does, the lamb stalks her and frightens the children.*

How would the accompaniment change to reflect each SUBTEXT? Perhaps the 2nd SUBTEXT would be more effective in a minor key or at a slower tempo.

6. *Watch music videos in a variety of styles. Notice how the director/producer/writer uses the images to enhance the music. Are the images literally reflecting the words, or is the video designed to reflect a mood?*

7. *Instead of taking the musical underscore in a film for granted, listen to how the composer enhances the action. Is the music creating a particular mood? Does the music forecast something the characters aren't even aware of? What happens to the music during chase scenes, love scenes, or moments of terror?*

Chapter 12

THE WANT

Want it, Need it, Gotta Have it

Everyone has heard the acting cliché, "What's my motivation?" This question is important because your motivation is what causes you to respond, to react. For example, winning the lottery might motivate you to scream and jump out of your seat, whereas receiving an outrageous electric bill might motivate you sit in your chair and sulk.

Your motivation is profoundly influenced by your WANTS and needs. It is your wants and needs that "motivate" you to act and react in a certain way. It also determines *to what degree* you react. WANT can also be described using more emotional words, such as "need," "desire," or "yearn for."

> *"In 'real life,' the mother begging for her child's life, the criminal begging for a pardon...these people give no attention whatever to their own state, and all attention to the state of that person from whom they require their object."* **David Mamet**

As an actor, you should ask yourself "What do I WANT?" before you dig into a song, a scene, or a role. For example, if you are playing the character, J. Pierrepont Finch, in *How to Succeed in Business,* you should ask, "What do I want from this job?" In the musical, *Wicked,* if playing Elphaba you might ask "What am I yearning for when I meet the Wizard?", and if playing Cathy in *The Last Five Years,* you may find it quite helpful to ask, "What do I need from my husband in this marriage?"

ACTION WORDS

Because "want" is just a feeling, it's better to use action words to express your WANT. Why? Because action words are "to do" words, and acting is an active ("to do") endeavor. This is where your OBJECTIVE comes in. What do you want TO DO about this want? This OBJECTIVE assures that there will be DRAMATIC ACTION rather than just a lovesick look or a forlorn grimace. "I *want* to be happy at work (a feeling), so I will ask my boss for a raise and demand a vacation (active choices.)" Even the most benign feelings must be played actively. You can *feel* bored but on stage you will need to actually express it through your DRAMATIC ACTION. Therefore, your OBJECTIVE will be to express your displeasure whenever someone asks a question that extends the boring lecture you're attending. This need for action does not give you permission to over-react. Instead, it should simply inspire you to honestly and naturally inform your audience of your emotional state as you fulfill an intention.

> *"You can't play an emotional condition; you have an emotional condition, and because you have that condition, you try to overcome it with active doings (intentions)."*
> **Larry Moss**

THE ENSEMBLE IS NO EXCEPTION

Determining a WANT and an OBJECTIVE is not just a requirement for the leads. Each member of the ensemble must be aware of his or her WANTS as well. If the ensemble members in *The Music Man* merely bob their heads and repeat, "watermelon, rhubarb" over and over again, there will be no honest relationships in the town of River City. However, if each actor can create relationships based on their WANTS, the town will come alive. ("I want to ask you for your apple pie recipe" or "I want you to help me track down my son who was last seen in the pool hall."). The audience will be watching a real town, with real people, not just a sea of humanity that happens to provide vocal harmonies. Individual WANTS are as vital in River City as they are in Anatevka, or at a party in the home of the Von Trapps.

> **NOTE: Remember to be aware of your reactions while you are playing out the WANTS and OBJECTIVES in your own life. (Acting is remembering what we did when we felt a certain way.) Did you bite your lip while you were waiting outside the principal's office? Did your voice quiver when you asked for your fiancé's hand in marriage? Did you slam the door when you found out you failed your driving test? (You really *wanted* to pass!)**

THE WANT AND THE BEFORE

A character's WANTS are directly affected by what has happened BEFORE. This can be a BEFORE that has just occurred or one that has been many years in the making. Your character may WANT to be the center of attention to show off an outrageous new outfit. However, the broader WANT may have more to do with the need for acceptance after having suffered abandonment as a child. The script may only infer a broader WANT, but, as an actor, you can basically work backwards to fill in a broader series of BACKSTORY events that have motivated the character's current actions. In *Carousel,* we may not know the whole story of Billy Bigelow's youth, but we can safely assume that

159

many of his WANTS and OBJECTIVES come from a long, dysfunctional background.

> *"I have learned over the years that pretty much any successful musical you can name has an "I Want" song for its main character within the first fifteen or so minutes of the show..."Just Around the Riverbend" [from Pocahontas] may not be a classic "I want" song, because the character doesn't really want anything that strongly until she meets John Smith, but it sets up her sense that she has another destiny to pursue than the one laid out for her by her father and society and her desire to go after it."*
>
> *Stephen Schwartz*

REINVENTING A SONG THROUGH WANT

As singers, we often take a song from a musical out of context for a concert or cabaret setting. Sometimes we may perform songs with no theatrical context at all. Either way, it's useful to come up with a BACKSTORY and WANTS to give depth to a song.

Sometimes it's fun to reinvent a song by changing the circumstances, the BACKSTORY, the WHOM, and/or the WANT. For example, in the song, "I Really Like Him," from *Man of La Mancha*, Sancho sings about his experiences with, and his love for, his master, Don Quixote. He wants the world to know that he will follow Quixote in spite of his master's eccentric behavior.

Since I've been with him
Cuckoo-nuts have been in season
But there's nothing I can do,
Chop me up for onion stew

160

Still I'll yell to the sky
Though I can't tell you why
That I like him.

As a singer, you can change the character's gender as well as the circumstances, the BACKSTORY, the WANTS, and the OBJECTIVES to give the song a whole new meaning without changing a note or lyric. For example:

The new CHARACTER and BACKSTORY: "I'm a single woman in my late thirties with a stressful job who has been dating for years without much luck. However, for the last three weeks, I've been seeing this crazy guy who makes me laugh, and when I'm with him, even though people think he's a little strange, I forget about all of my problems."

WANT: "I want my friends and family to accept him, 'because I like him. I really like him.' "

OBJECTIVE: Even though I can't logically explain it, I will still tell all of my skeptical friends and family how much I care about him. I will convince them that he's the best thing that's happened to me in a long time.

Same music, same lyrics, with a fresh approach.

"The aim of art is to represent not the outward appearance of things, but their inward significance."
                                      Aristotle

HOW TO MAKE THE STRONGEST CHOICE

Your WANT can change from scene to scene as well as moment to moment. This keeps your performance alive and honest. If your WANT is exactly the same in every moment throughout the song, you run the risk of playing an attitude rather than a person. You may WANT to stomp into your boss' office and quit, but the moment he answers your angry knock, you decide, instead, that you WANT to pay your bills. Your WANT and your DRAMATIC ACTION has changed in one small moment.

We all have contrasting emotions from moment to moment. That's how we smile through the tears and laugh through the pain. That's also how we keep our audience engaged. If we play a scene or song as sad, very sad, and very, very sad, it's a little like eating a five-course meal of nothing but ever-increasing servings of pasta—no appetizer to tease our senses for what's to come and no contrasting flavors to look forward to.

> *"Any intelligent fool can make things bigger, more complex, and more violent. It takes a touch of genius—and a lot of courage—to move in the opposite direction."*
> *Albert Einstein*

In the song, "I Dreamed a Dream" from *Les Miserables,* the actor playing Fantine can either play the angst throughout the entire song, or she can offer a richer fabric of feelings. Fantine WANTS to be happy and secure in spite of her tragic circumstances. She WANTS this because she remembers what happiness felt like. If she gives us, the audience, a glimpse of the happiness that once was ("He spent a summer by my side. He filled my days with endless wonder"), then we are even more devastated for her when she succumbs to the misery of what is. ("But he was gone when autumn came").

TRANSITION AND WANT

A good composer/lyricist recognizes the value of a good musical and theatrical TRANSITION, and this TRANSITION usually marks a change in the character's WANT. In "Just You Wait, Henry Higgins" (*My Fair Lady*), Lerner and Loewe successfully marry the aggressive text and music when Eliza WANTS to make Henry Higgins pay for his arrogance and abuse. ("When you yell you're gonna drown, I'll get dressed and go to town.") In the middle of the song, however, she WANTS something else, and the music and the text reflect this. The accompaniment becomes more refined and delicate as she sings, "One day I'll be famous. I'll be proper and prim." Here, she WANTS to be a lady that is respected by society more than she WANTS Henry Higgins' head. That, of course, is followed by another TRANSITION that takes her back to her original WANT. ("Then they'll march you, Henry Higgins, to the wall!")

SUBTEXT AND WANT

What you *really* mean is directly related to what you *really* want. Therefore, your SUBTEXT and your WANT are connected. In the *Sound of Music*, when the Mother Abbess sings "Climb Every Mountain" to Maria, she WANTS Maria to have courage and return to the Von Trapp household to face her feelings about the Captain. Therefore her OBJECTIVE reflects her SUBTEXT: "I will tell her not to give up. I will convince her that she must follow every path possible until she fulfills her dreams." This WANT, OBJECTIVE, and SUBTEXT remain the same even when the circumstances change. For example, when The Mother Abbess sings the reprise of the song, she still wants Maria to have courage and follow her dreams as she encourages her to flee her home to escape the Nazis.

PROGRESSION AND WANT

A changing intensity in the WANT provides a natural acting PROGRESSION. This isn't the same as sobbing harder and harder as the song or scene unfolds. It's more about uping the stakes in a moment by moment way.

For example: (On the phone with a friend.)

"I WANT to see you after work. Why don't we walk home together so we can talk?"

(Your friend is late, the office is closed, and it's getting dark. You call and leave a message.)

"Hey, it's getting dark, and I'd sure feel safer walking home with a friend."

(Now, it's after dark and there are some unsavory characters showing up.)

"I'm getting worried. Where are you? I WANT to make it home in one piece before something bad happens!"

Keeping your focus on the external IMAGES and successive WANTS will evoke a more honest reaction than if you simply decide to "act" more and more scared. This growing WANT will be directly affected by your OBSTACLES—your friend's tardiness, the dark, and the threatening environment. (The

OBSTACLE is another vital component of FORM that is discussed in the next chapter.)

EXERCISES

Because the WANT and the OBSTACLE are tied so closely together, the exercises for this chapter are at the end of the next chapter (Chapter 13--THE OBSTACLE).

Chapter 13

THE OBSTACLE

Push Me, Pull Me

> "An actor is looking for conflict. Conflict is what creates drama. We are taught to avoid trouble [so] actors don't realize they must go looking for it. The more conflict actors find, the more interesting the performance."
>
> Michael Shurtleff

OBSTACLE

In the musical, *Dreamgirls*, the character, Effie, has been unfairly replaced as one of the singers in a successful female trio. She appeals to Curtis, her former lover and the manager of the group, who has not only replaced her in the group, but has replaced her with someone else in his life. In the song, "And I am Telling You I'm Not Going," Effie wants to be in the group, and, more importantly, she desperately wants Curtis back. Her WANT grows more and more passionate as she is met with more and more resistance from Curtis, a man she still loves. The song grows from frustrated WANT to desperate need, and ends with a final outcry of defiance. In this song, her WANT and her OBJECTIVE are directly affected by her OBSTACLE (Curtis).

Just as there are opposing forces in nature, there are opposing forces in our emotional lives. In a game of tug-of-war, there is always tension between these two forces, even

167

though one side may briefly overtake another. In a dramatic work, every WANT must also have an opposing force, an OBSTACLE. This OBSTACLE gives your character something to push against, something to fight for. These opposing forces are your best tool for giving feeling FORM because they are what maintain the balance between the tension and release.

> *"The more constraints one imposes, the more one frees oneself. "*
> *Igor Stravinsky*

WHAT'S IN MY WAY?

When doing a role, the actor must first ask the question, "What do I WANT?" In order to establish the OBSTACLE, this should immediately be followed by the question, "What's in my way?" Think of the classic WANTS and OBSTACLES of various fairy tale characters: Cinderella, Red Riding Hood, Rapunzel, and Jack, of beanstalk fame. (Sondheim brilliantly deals with the traditional - and not so traditional - WANTS and OBSTACLES of these characters in his musical *Into the Woods.*) Your conflicts, or OBSTACLES, will not always be the physical kind (a stepmother, a wolf, or a giant), but may, instead, be moral and ethical ones. You WANT your teacher to give you an "A" because it will give you a leg-up into the best college, but there is a conflict, an OBSTACLE. You didn't really write the paper you have submitted to be graded. Your OBSTACLE is a moral one. What's in your way? Your own conscience, your sense of right and wrong.

WHAT AM I WILLING TO DO TO GET IT?

After asking "What's in my way?" you should ask "What am I willing to do to get what I want?" in order to determine the degree of your DRAMATIC ACTION. This question doesn't imply that you should always "give it your all." Sometimes the character and the situation call for a more nuanced choice. You may not always go for the jugular in order to get what you want. There may be a more gentle "push and pull" in certain circumstances. In *Fiddler on the Roof,* Tevye, at first, casually deals with the everyday back and forth struggle between "one hand" and "the other hand." The tension mounts, however, when Tevye is increasingly faced with more pressing OBSTACLES. The stakes are highest when his daughter, Chava, decides to marry outside of the faith. He WANTS to love and accept her, but he now faces his greatest OBSTACLE, her marriage, a marriage that goes against everything he believes in. This is where the tension between his WANT and the OBSTACLE peaks.

What do I want, and what am I willing to do to get what I want? Cinderella is willing to defy her stepmother in order to go to the ball. Red Riding Hood is willing to face danger in the woods to see her grandmother. Prince Charming is willing to go to every home in every village to find Cinderella. Each character struggles with the balance between WANT and OBSTACLE, and this struggle is what fuels the theatrical fire.

"The absence of limitations is the enemy of art."
                                                 Orson Welles

---

NOTE: Think of your daily life as a combination of WANT and "can't have" OBSTACLES. You want to have time in the bathroom to get ready for school, but you can't because your sister won't let you in. You may not be willing to kick the door down, but you might be willing to bargain with her. You want a piece of cheesecake, but you can't because you'll gain the weight you've worked so hard to lose. You may be willing to give up the cheesecake or you may not, giving in "just this once." You'll be amazed how many times in a day you face these opposing forces.

IMAGERY AND YOUR OBSTACLES

Don't forget that your IMAGERY choices are excellent sources for the conflict between WANT and OBSTACLE. This is where THE WINE and THE BOTTLE come together.

> Your WHOM: (Unrequited love is one of the most popular theatrical conflicts). "I WANT you to love me, but you love someone else."

> Your WHERE: (The elements—rain, wind, gravity, pollution.) "I WANT to go on a picnic, but it's raining today."

> Your WHEN: (Who ever has enough time to accomplish a WANT?) "I WANT to get this report done, but it's due before I'll have time to do the research."

Your INNER IMAGES: (The guilt of past mistakes, the fear of future ones.) "I WANT to start a new job, but the last time I quit, it took a year to find a position."

Besides the fourth-wall IMAGERY, you will also have fellow actors on stage with you, and a score and a script that will provide you with additional WANTS and OBSTACLES.

> *"An actor must make his needs (goals, wants, objectives) so strong that he is willing to interfere with the other actor in order to get what he needs. Interfering means getting in their way so that what you want is stronger than what they want."*　　　　　*Michael Shurtleff*

COUNTERWEIGHT

Creativity is about making the strongest CHOICE. Sometimes, however, the loudest, most intense, most angst-driven choice isn't the "strongest" one. Sometimes, playing *against* the most obvious choice is effective. This COUNTERWEIGHT can ultimately provide even more intensity in a song or scene. For example, the whispered energy of a ghost story, or the maybe-I'll-tell-you-later attitude before sharing a juicy piece of gossip can create an effective tension for you and your audience. Even the overwhelming WANTS and OBSTACLES that are associated with the intense feelings of love, can be expressed in a variety of ways, depending on the context, the characters, and the SUBTEXT. Love can be shouted with loud exuberance ala "I'm in Love With a Wonderful Guy" (*South Pacific)*, or reflected on with quiet intensity, as in "A Quiet Thing" (*Flora, the Red Menace)*. This is why a once-size-fits-all posture and delivery won't provide you with the strongest choices.

171

MUSICAL FORM/DRAMATIC FORM

The acting singer must always consider both the music and the acting when making artistic choices. This will require listening to the FORM of a song and making acting choices accordingly. Most theatrical songs are in AB FORM, ABA FORM, or they are THROUGH-COMPOSED. AB FORM is when there is a musical statement followed by a departure from that statement. For the actor, this implies a change of heart, or a change of WANT and OBSTACLE. ABA FORM includes the departure that exists in AB form, but there is a musical return to the opening before the piece is over. In most theatrical music, however, this return has a slightly altered dramatic context. Either the opening WANT and OBSTACLE is intensified, or it takes on a brand new perspective. In a THROUGH-COMPOSED piece, the music follows the ebb and flow, the WANTS and OBSTACLES, of the text without a specific A or B section.

AB FORM

In Billy Bigalow's "Soliloquy" from *Carousel* there is a musical and acting transition that changes the WANT and OBSTACLE.

THE A SECTION
I can see him when he's seventeen or so,
And startin' to go with a girl
I can give him lots of pointers, very sound
On the way to get 'round any girl
I can tell him ...

Here, there is a transition, a departure. His WANT and OBSTACLE changes.

172

THE **B** SECTION
> *Wait a minute!*
> *Could it be?*
> *What the hell!*
> *What if he is a girl?*
> *What would I do with her?*
> *What could I do for her?*
> *A bum with no money!*
> *You can have fun with a son*
> *But you gotta be a father to a girl*

ABA FORM

THE **A** SECTION
> In the A section of the song "Gethsemane" from *Jesus Christ Superstar*, Jesus WANTS to know if there is a way around the OBSTACLE, a "way to take this cup away from me for I don't want to taste its poison".

THE **B** SECTION
> In the B section, the music and the lyrics are more contemplative and improvisational as Jesus WANTS to know "why should I die?" His OBSTACLE isn't as much God as his own internal struggle. There is then a musical and emotional TRANSITION that includes a musical and acting BEAT, a pause, a make-the-audience-wait moment of tension before the return of the original theme.

THE RETURN TO THE **A** SECTION
> This time, the A section music is essentially the same melody as before, but it is higher and more intense. At this point, there is a giving-in to the OBSTACLE, a release of the tension.

God, thy will is hard
But you hold every card
I will drink your cup of poison
Nail me to your cross
And break me, bleed me, beat me
Kill me, take me now
Before I change my mind.

("Time" is now his OBSTACLE as he asks God to "take me before I change my mind.")

THROUGH-COMPOSED

If you listen to "Bohemian Rhapsody" by Queen you will hear how the music is composed to suit the ever-changing lyrics. Not only does the composition, the tone, and the tempo change to suit the text, but so does the basic style. The song uses everything from four-part a cappella harmony, to opera-like melodies, to driving hard rock, all accompanying a somewhat confusing but rich text. This is all done without a returning chorus and other components of standard pop form.

UNPREDICTABILITY = FEELING

As you've learned, change and COUNTERWEIGHT are effective tools for FEELING and FORM. So too is unpredictability. Shaking up expectations, whether it's with song form or emotional content is a great tool for eliciting feeling from your audience. If your audience is expecting a return to the original theme, but you suddenly (but justifiably) take off in a different direction, you're likely to get their attention. The same is true with your acting choices. If your audience is set up to expect an outburst, but you offer a moment of silence instead, there may be an improved "goosebump" factor.

For example, imagine yourself as a teenager who has arrived home after staying out way past curfew. You expect a loud and angry lecture from your father who has been waiting up. However, if this time your dad quietly takes his glasses off, puts his magazine down, and goes to bed without a word, you will probably feel twice as guilty about staying out late. He has shaken your expectations and heightened your shame. Your dad made a strong choice for the moment, and it wasn't the loud one you expected.

THE END

The conclusion of a song or monologue should be the culmination of everything that has come before. Every musical and dramatic TRANSITION and PROGRESSION leads up to this moment. It can be a "shout it from the mountain tops" ending or a sweet epilogue of realization. You must remember that the song isn't over until the last note of the accompaniment. The musical SUBTEXT is still alive even when you are not singing, so you owe it to your audience to maintain the fantasy and the emotional intensity all the way to the end, and even a little beyond. The audience members must feel that life will go on after this moment, that there is a sequel out there somewhere.

ENDING CLICHES

The jazz-hands ending button can look exciting, but if we've seen it a hundred times, it simply loses its effectiveness. Why not "button" an up-tempo with a wink and a nod or a look of shock instead a pair of jazz hands? Even if you are choreographed with jazz hands at the end of the number, it's your job to make it effective by connecting it with your IMAGERY and your OBJECTIVE. And, for heaven's sake, resist using the cliché upturned palms (unless you're Oliver asking, "Please sir, may I have some more?")

> *"It is well that the earth is round that we do not see too far ahead."*
> *Meryl Streep*

AVOID FORCASTING THE ENDING

It's tempting sometimes to play the angst or the joy of the ending too soon. You can avoid this if you remember to maintain moment-to-moment WANTS and OBSTACLES. The audience doesn't want to know how it all ends, even if they've seen the musical seven times. They want to watch you experience each moment for the first time as the story unfolds, and you, the actor, must do just that. If you are engaged in your IMAGERY and are committed to your WANTS and OBSTACLES, moment by moment, this probably won't be a problem.

PUTTING IT TOGETHER

Just like the sculptor sets the image free by chiseling the marble, you will chip away at a song or scene until an artistic whole emerges. This process can be frustrating in our problem/solution world, but creativity rarely happens in apple-pie order. It's more a matter of chipping away, gathering and experimenting, until a pattern emerges. This means that you must be willing to let go. It will require you to live with things that are unresolved and undone until you've had a chance to flush things out in the rehearsal process. Eventually, however, after lots of trial-and-error, you will put it all together. Stephen Sondheim says it best in his song, "Putting it Together" from *Sunday in the Park with George:*

> *Bit by bit, putting it together*
> *Piece by piece, only way to make a work of art*
> *Every moment makes a contribution*
> *Every little detail plays a part.*

THE INGREDIENTS FOR YOUR KITCHEN

Think of the choices you can make (using the principles of IMAGERY, SENSE MEMORY, and FORM) as the ingredients and recipes for a dinner. Let the following metaphor simply wash over you.

> *You have a general idea of what you want to serve on the menu based on your guests and the surrounding circumstances of the event. You plan a basic menu and go shopping for the ingredients. However, as you shop, you consider additional recipes and ingredients. When you get home you have bags of food items. Some you will use, and some you may put away for another day. You may even be inspired to try out a few new recipes. Some you will reject, but some will pleasantly surprise you. (You simply can't use the same recipe for each dish since each dish will be a unique combination of ingredients.) Eventually, you will decide on the best recipes and their respective ingredients. You will then put the various dishes on your menu in order of presentation—appetizers, the main course, dessert. (You may even make a few adjustments after the guests arrive.)*

The point? You must look at the whole before you dig into the parts. Then, you must continually allow for a change in plans as you keep your eye on the ultimate goal—a delicious, cohesive, and tasty "meal."

SUMMING IT ALL UP

The following questions are included to guide your process of discovery. They are not a step-by-step approach to acting, so don't worry about the order. They are simply designed to help you do the "chipping away and the gathering" before a performance. They may even provide you with ideas for a future performance instead of the performance at hand. Nothing in art is wasted. Some lesser choices are there to help you find the best choices. Some excellent choices that are not necessarily right for one performance may be perfect for another.

Think of the following questions as a study guide or a homework assignment that will ultimately help you navigate a course. There is simply no way to hold on to all of these questions and answers during performance. Although they are vital for your preparation, they should be put away in performance so that you can allow yourself the free flow of expression while living in the fantasy of the moment.

WHO AM I?

WHAT ARE THE CIRCUMSTANCES?

TO WHOM AM I SINGING?

WHERE AM I?

WHAT TIME IS IT?

*(Your **INNER IMAGES** will flourish when you ask the following questions.).*

WHAT IS MY BACKSTORY? - (LONGTERM, RECENT, and THE MOMENT BEFORE. *(This will help explain the circumstances, the **WHY**)*

WHAT DO I WANT?

WHAT WILL I DO TO FULFILL THIS WANT? *(My **OBJECTIVE**)*

WHAT IS IN MY WAY? *(My **OBSTACLE**)*

WHAT AM I WILLING TO DO TO GET WHAT I WANT?

AN EXAMPLE OF THIS PROCESS:

WHO AM I? *I am a 21-year-old female with a great body, a nice face, and pretty hair. (The rest of the description will be in the BACKSTORY).*

WHAT ARE THE CIRCUMSTANCES? *(These are directly related to the BACKSTORY) I am one of the finalists in the Miss Nevada Royale Beauty Contest, but my talent portion of the pageant didn't go well. I have been accused of cheating.*

TO WHOM AM I SINGING? *To the judges of the Miss Nevada Royale Beauty Contest. Specifically, to the pageant director who is a 50-something, self-righteous former beauty queen (from the character's perspective anyway).*

WHERE AM I? *Backstage at the pageant theatre, a dusty old building in Reno, Nevada with bad lighting and peeling paint.*

WHAT TIME IS IT? *It's an hour into the final performance. In fact, it's intermission, but it's running long due to the circumstances.*

*(Your **INNER IMAGES** will flourish when you ask the following questions.).*

WHAT IS MY BACKSTORY?

LONGTERM: *I was raised on a ranch by a single mother. As the youngest of five children, and the prettiest, I was told that I would be the one to bring the family out of poverty. I've never felt very popular, but I want to be. I want to be famous and have the power to change things.*

RECENT: *I've worked out every day, changed my wardrobe, and I've had a little work done on my nose so that I can compete in various beauty pageants, including the Miss Nevada Royale. Unfortunately, I just performed and my talent portion of the competition didn't go as well as I wanted, so I have to make up for it in the bathing suit competition. Miss Reno is my toughest competitor and she may have beat me in the talent portion already. I had to do something, so I just hid Miss Reno's bathing suit so she'll have to wear her shapeless exercise suit.*

MOMENT BEFORE: *(In this case, ask this after WHAT'S IN MY WAY.)*

WHAT DO I WANT? *I want to leave my life of poverty and boredom. I want to make something of myself. I want to win.*

WHAT WILL I DO TO FULFILL THIS WANT? *(My OBJECTIVE) I will hide the suit and win the competition.*

WHAT IS IN MY WAY? *(My OBSTACLE) Miss Reno and the judges who just found the suit in my dressing room.*

THE MOMENT BEFORE: *The judges are standing in front of me waiting for an explanation.*

WHAT AM I WILLING TO DO TO GET WHAT I WANT?
I will lie about the bathing suit, and tell them I had nothing to do with it.

> **NOTE: DON'T WORRY ABOUT THE ORDER OF THE QUESTIONS OR A PARTICULAR FORMAT. SIMPLY USE THE QUESTIONS TO INFORM YOUR CHOICES.**

EXERCISES

1. *Keep a journal of your own daily WANTS, OBJECTIVES, and OBSTACLES. What do you want? And what's in your way? What do you do to get what you want? Which WANTS and OBSTACLES affect you the most? (Sometimes it's the little irritations that will really get to you.)*

2. *Use a partner for this WANT exercise. Without using words (only nonsense sounds or a repeated phrase like "peanut butter"), use only your body language and vocal inflection to try and get your scene partner to guess what you want. (No indicating allowed!)*

   > *I want you to FORGIVE ME.*
   > *I want you to BELIEVE IN ME.*
   > *I want you to LEAVE WITH ME.*
   > *I want you to DO MY CHORES FOR ME. (No Charades!)*

Make up your own WANTS to use in this exercise, basing them on something that has happened during your day.

3. *Create a short monologue that takes into account your WANTS, OBJECTIVES and OBSTACLES and uses WHOM, WHERE, and INNER IMAGERY. Make sure you include a BEFORE as well. Eventually put it in conversational form.*

   *Identify the **WHOM, WHERE, BEFORE, WANT, OBJECTIVE, and OBSTACLE** in the following example before you create your own monologue;*

   I wish I had worn a coat today. Who knew the weather would turn out like this in the middle of April? Where is my friend? I've been waiting for him for over an hour. Oh, there he is. Finally! I'm freezing and I'm mad. I just want to get home so I can take a long hot shower. I'm sure going to give him a piece of my mind.

   "Thanks for finally showing up, Mike. Let's just get out of here. I'm miserable...What? You didn't bring the car? Are you kidding me? We're going to have to wait another hour for the bus!"

4. *Fill in the following **feeling** with a **WANT** sentence. Follow that with an **OBJECTIVE**.*

   For example:

   *I **feel** happy that it's my friend's birthday.*
   *I **want** to celebrate.*
   *I will **bake** a cake and **present it** to her.*

*I **feel** gloomy on this rainy day.*
WANT:
OBJECTIVE:

*I **feel** silly in this cow costume.*
WANT:
OBJECTIVE:

Now make up your own feeling, WANT, and OBJECTIVE.

5. *Now try Exercise #4 using various songs.*

For example: "Tonight" from West Side Story.

*I **feel** happy that I am in love with Maria.*
*I **want** to see her.*
*I will **show up** at her apartment and **climb** her fire escape.*

NOTE: It's best to choose a pro-active action rather than a negative one. For example: Instead of "I don't want to be alone", choose "I want to be with her."

---

6. *This time, try Exercise #4 and #5, but add your OBSTACLES. What are you willing to do to overcome your OBSTACLES? To what degree?*

For example: "Tonight" from West Side Story.

*I **feel** happy that I am in love with Maria.*
*I **want** to see her.*
*I will **show up** at her apartment and **climb** her fire escape.*

183

YOUR OBSTACLES:

It's late at night and someone might see me in a neighborhood of people who may hate me. I'll take that chance since no one will probably see me. Besides it's worth it if I get to hold her.

Her papa may overhear us and throw me out or call the police, but I'm willing to take that risk. However, it might also get Maria is trouble, so I will say "goodnight" and plan to see her another time.

7. *Answer all of the questions in the final summary of Chapter 13. Base your answers on a song you've selected from the following WANT/OBSTACLE repertoire list. (Don't worry about the order of the questions or if certain questions overlap. The questions are simply there to help you make acting choices.)*

WHO AM I?

WHAT ARE THE CIRCUMSTANCES?

TO WHOM AM I SINGING?

WHERE AM I?

WHAT TIME IS IT?

*(Your **INNER IMAGES** will flourish when you ask the following questions.).*

WHAT IS MY BACKSTORY? *(Longterm, recent, and THE MOMENT BEFORE. This will also provide the Circumstances, the **WHY**.)*

WHAT DO I WANT?

WHAT WILL I DO TO FULFILL THIS WANT? *(My **OBJECTIVE**)*

WHAT IS IN MY WAY? *(My **OBSTACLE**)*

WHAT AM I WILLING TO DO TO GET WHAT I WANT?

WANT/OBSTACLE - Practice Repertoire

Adelaide's Lament	(*Guys And Dolls*) F. Loesser
And I Am Telling You	(*Dreamgirls*) - H. Krieger/ T. Eyen
Anyone Can Whistle	(*Anyone Can Whistle*) S. Sondheim
Astonishing	(*Little Women*) J. Howland/ M. Dickstein
Before The Parade Passes By	(*Hello Dolly*) J. Herman
Best	(*A Day in Hollywoord/A Night in the Ukraine*) F. Lazaruss/D.Viosburgh
Buddy's Blues	(*Follies*) S. Sondheim
Corner Of The Sky	(*Pippin*) S. Schwartz
Defying Gravity	(*Wicked*) S. Schwartz
I Have Confidence	(*The Sound of Music*) R. Rodgers/O. Hammerstein
I Hope I Get It	(*Chorus Line*) M. Hamlisch/ E. Kleban
I'm Not At All In Love	(*The Pajama Game*) R. Adler/J. Ross
King Of The World	(*Songs For A New World*) J.R. Brown
Matchmaker	(*Fiddler On The Roof*) J. Bock/S. Harnick
Maybe I Like It This Way	(*The Wild Party*) A. Lippa
Mister Cellophane	(*Chicago*) J. Kander/F. Ebb

On The Steps Of The Palace

(Into The Woods)
S. Sondheim

She Cries

(Songs for a New World)
J. R. Brown

Soliloquy

(Carousel) R. Rodgers/
O. Hammerstein

So Long Dearie

(Hello Dolly) J. Herman

Sometimes a Day Goes By

(Woman of the Year)-
J. Kander/F. Ebb

Raunchy

(110 in the Shade)
H. Schmidt/T. Jones

Take A Chance On Me

(Little Women) J. Howland/
M. Dickstein

Whatever Lola Wants

(Damn Yankees) R. Adler/
J. Ross

Where I Want To Be

(Chess) B. Andersson/
B. Ulvaeus/R. Rice

Who Will Love Me As I Am

(Sideshow) B. Russell/
H. Krieger

You Don't Know This Man

(Parade) J.R. Brown

Chapter 14

STYLE

Feeling in Another Frame

"Style is a journey from tourist to native. It is living in the world of the play, not just visiting it."
                                                    Robert Barton

---

For the singer, the word, "style," is used in a variety of ways. It may refer to an era, as in "classical style vs. contemporary style," or it may refer to a particular genre, such as "jazz style" or "pop style." It also refers to the unique way you may express a song of any style, your "personal style." Although good vocal and acting techniques can serve as a foundation for all of these definitions, there are many other considerations that must be taken into account when you perform in a certain style. Such things as vocal color, phrasing, diction, and physical delivery will vary considerably from style to style, so the more flexible you are as a singer and an actor, the more adaptable you will be when it comes to style. On the other hand, it's also important to realize that your physical type and voice may be better suited to one style than another.

"Art begins in imitation and ends in innovation."
                                                    Mason Cooley

---

IMITATION, THE SINCEREST FORM OF FLATTERY

The best way to learn to sing in a particular style is to listen to those who have mastered that style. Depending on your ability and interests, listening and imitating will probably initially teach you more than learning the "rules" of a particular style. Eventually, after you've listened to a variety of artists within a style (to avoid becoming a clone of just one), you will want to make your own decisions in order to develop your own style. Just keep in mind that some styles are more flexible than others when it comes to individual interpretation. For example, opera has little individual flexibility while the improvisational nature of jazz requires it.

> *"In the theatre we reach out and touch the past through literature, history and memory so that we might receive and relive significant and relevant human qualities in the present and then pass them on to future generations."*
> *Anne Bogart*

UNDERSTANDING HISTORY

Contemporary music and acting styles are fairly easy to imitate and understand since they reflect the times we live in, but if you want to perform a work from a different era with integrity, you will need to understand the times the work was conceived in. For example, if you lived in the world of the 18th century royal elites, you might identify with the magnificent operas and elaborate sets that reflected a life of opulence. You probably would have admired the storylines about mythical gods while reveling in the flirtatious romps that reflected the lifestyles of these elites. On the other hand, if you lived a Bohemian lifestyle in a modest flat in 19th century Europe, the Romantic period's ill-fated love affairs and suffering would have been more relevant to your life.

For the performing artist, understanding history and culture requires more than memorizing dates and rattling off the names of generals and inventors. These facts are only relevant if you understand how they affect the person living in the time. It's the details of everyday life--details that are certainly affected by wars and inventions--that will better inform your acting choices. For example, the flirtatious language of a silk fan may have great significance in one era, while giving someone your phone number has implications in another.

In spite of the differences from era to era, there is one common thread that doesn't change throughout the course of history, and that is human emotion. Love, passion, jealousy and rage are all a permanent part of the human condition. It is only the expression of these feelings that varies. Social, cultural, and political environments may frame human emotion differently, but whether it's Shakespeare or Sondheim, love is love, and hate is hate.

THINGS NEVER CHANGE

The fundamental tools for singing and acting provide a good foundation for any style, but there must also be a process that allows you to understand the expression of feeling in a particular era. Although you can use the tools of IMAGERY and FORM to express jealousy (and everyone knows what jealousy feels like), you will have to take into account how that jealousy might have been expressed in relation to the period. For example, is the jealousy expressed on Facebook or by challenging someone to a duel? Throughout time, love has been fallen in and out of, but a young woman who must marry a man she's never met to save a kingdom may have a different reaction than a contemporary businesswoman who doesn't want to upset her parents because she's marrying the drummer in a rock band.

> *"Mankind is so much the same, in all times and places, that history informs us of nothing new or strange in this particular. Its chief use is only to discover the constant and universal principles of human nature."*
>
> *David Hume*

WHAT IF and SUBSTITUTION

You may not relate much to the 17th Century guy who is preparing for a duel or the 17th Century woman who is promised to a king she has never met. You can, however, relate to their feelings of jealousy or despair by using the WHAT IF with a healthy dose of SUBSTITUTION from your own life and times. You can imagine how your body would react if you thought you were going to die in a duel, and you can probably relate to the pressure of not wanting to disappoint your parents. That won't be enough, but it's a start. The rest will require some homework if you are going to be able to connect to the intensity, the urgency, and the enormity of a situation that occurs in a particular time period. For example, you must understand the attitudes in the 1940's to fully appreciate the themes of prejudice in Rodgers and Hammerstein's musical, *South Pacific.* You must also acknowledge and respond to the devastating effects a queen's affair with the king's knight would have had on a royal kingdom in the Middle Ages to appreciate the conflict in Lerner and Loewe's *Camelot.*

IMMERSE YOURSELF

In order to fully understand a period of time, you must immerse yourself in it. It's a great idea to look at period paintings, listen to period music, explore old photos, and visit a variety of museums. Read poetry, novels, and diaries, and study the attire and social customs of an era. Get a "feel" for a time by watching period movies with authentic production value, such as *Anna Karenina*, *Les Miserables*, *Dangerous Liaisons, or Titanic*.

Imagine the day-to-day life of an individual in a particular era or culture. What did it take to prepare a meal? What were the rituals of courtship? How did you keep warm or cool? What was it like to get dressed in the morning? What were the medical risks of the flu, a wound, or childbirth? The communication limitations of a particular era may have made a goodbye even more poignant. A lack of antibiotics may have made an illness more devastating, and the lack of opportunities for a woman might have made a marriage proposal even more vital.

> **NOTE: One of the best references for the actor when it comes to the expression of historical style is a book by Robert Barton called *Style for Actors--A Handbook for Moving Beyond Realism*. This and other books that provide an overview of performing arts history will give you a perspective and feel for various eras in history.**

AMERICAN HISTORY AND "STYLE"

The art of each era is influenced by the art of the previous one. Whether it's musical theatre, jazz, pop, rock, or country, we can trace our musical performance roots by studying our history as a country. The popular American music at the turn of the 20th Century was influenced by the European Romantic era melodies of the 19th century. The acting of this time, unfortunately, was characterized by over-the-top representational gestures. (Swooning with the back of the hand on the forehead or clutching one's heart.) In today's world, due to film and television, audiences demand a more intimate and natural style of acting, even when you are performing the music of a bygone era. Otherwise, you might leave your modern audience unaffected and confused. Because of this, you must find a balance between "then" and "now" when you perform. For example, the fast vibrato and sometimes transparent sound of the 1920's soprano has been respectfully adapted for the modern ear. Today's singers who perform repertoire from this era will probably have more core in the sound with more connection between the vocal bridges, but they must still sing with the melodic lyricism of the period. They will also probably replace some of the clichéd acting moves with a more contemporary approach, and, thanks to the wireless microphone, their speaking voices will probably be more natural and relaxed than they would have been projecting in a large auditorium without amplification.

THE 20's

The end of World War I ushered us into a modern world where women did away with the corset and gained the vote. By the 1920's, the operettas of Gilbert and Sullivan and Victor Herbert were being replaced with the unique and popular sounds of American jazz, a style that grew from ragtime and other African-American musical roots. The party atmosphere of the Roaring Twenties changed everything, from hem lines to dance moves. The romantic sentimentality remained from before, but now there was a new and naughty energy. The prohibition of alcohol made drinking even more desirable, and the Speakeasy was born. The popular music of the period spread to every home via vinyl and the radio, but the music and theatre of the time had one foot in the Romantic era of yesteryear and the other in the modern Jazz Age, as evidenced in Jerome Kern's musical, *Showboat.*

How does all of this affect the acting singer? The history of a period informs your theatrical and musical choices so that you can bring the artistic expression of the era to life. It also helps you understand the balance between "too little" and "too much." For example, in the 20's, syncopated jazz rhythms and decadent dances like The Charleston broke away from the reserved, old-fashioned music and dance of the past. Yet, there were still elements of the operetta alive and the sentimental romance of "boy meets girl, boy marries girl" remained. Both the up-tempo numbers and ballads of the era reflect this dichotomy. The musicals of the time were primarily a collection of popular songs with flimsy librettos, so the delivery of the songs and the dance numbers took precedence over the acting.

THE 30's

The economic crash of 1929 changed the world in one fell swoop. Although some of the music of the 30's reflected the despair of The Great Depression, the "talkies" provided a musical and theatrical escape from the dark times most people were experiencing. This opulence fantasy was evident in the movies of Fred Astaire and Ginger Rogers where the men wore top hats and tails and the women wore long gowns adorned with sequins and feathers. The movies of the time were all about dancing, from ballroom to tap, and the scripts had slightly more integrity than in the 20's, although most of them reflected a "we're in the money" attitude. The women were a little tougher in this period—

newspaper women and secretaries—until the men swept them off their feet (literally). Because of the popularity of film, the acting was somewhat more intimate, but, in the popular movie musicals of the period, the big production numbers still took precedence over the acting.

THE 40's

Another world war was brewing in the late 1930's, and Pearl Harbor brought it to the home front. Saying goodbye to a loved one who might never come home profoundly affected the acting and the music of the era. The microphone and film had already brought an intimacy to the acting, but now the singing and acting were even more personal. The vocal music was more connected to the speaking voice, and thus, most of the keys were lower than before. This also meant that the diction and vocal color were more closely connected to the American dialect with its diphthongs and elongated consonants. The slightly behind-the-beat phrasing and gentle scoops up to the pitch (precursors to the American pop style) also expressed the heartfelt lyrics of wartime goodbyes. The microphone was by now a permanent fixture for the singer as he or she crooned the ballads. Yet, as in any era, there was a contrast to these sentimental ballads, and that was the big band sound of Swing. Singers would scat along with the big band instruments that accompanied them, and what could have been more fun than dancing to this music with its acrobatic moves, especially when you felt the need to enjoy life while you still could.

THE 50's

During the 1950's, a carefree youth-oriented world was unconcerned with war (World War II was, after all, the "war to end all wars.") Although recordings had been around for some time, the commercial music business exploded in large part due to television. The driving beat of rock 'n' roll celebrated the same youthful energy of the 1920's, only in this era, rather than a woman's knees, Elvis' gyrating hips were the controversy. The singers often held the microphone in order to move while singing, and the lyrics served the energy of the music, rather than the other way around. Songs about puppy love and teen romance replaced many of the sultry ballads of the previous era. Just as in any other era, there was a balance. Even though this rock 'n roll era celebrated the brooding young delinquent (ala James Dean), the "boy meets girl, boy marries girl" traditions were still very much part of the culture. Unfortunately, this era has become a caricature of itself because of musicals like *Grease* and *All Shook Up*, but it is still popular thanks to its simplicity and fun. The acting singer should embrace this period with a certain "ah to heck with it" attitude. The voices were rarely trained, and the guitar players were usually out of tune, but it was the foundation for most of our pop music of today.

American musical theatre flourished during this decade, but the music reflected the popular styles of the 40's, not rock n' roll. Some of America's best loved musicals were written during the 1950's, including such classics as *Guys and Dolls* and *West Side Story*.

THE 60's

The 1960's marked a return to war without the patriotism and sense of responsibility that were a part of the 1940's. The frustration with the Vietnam War was met with either angry protest songs or a "drop out of society altogether" attitude. This led to a hippie counter culture that profoundly influenced the music scene. The harsh realities of the world were reflected in the distortion of the electronic accompaniments (ala Jimmy Hendrix) and that distorted sound also carried over to the singing voice (ala Janis Joplin).

Yet the peace movement's folk sound and the carefree attitude of free love ("love the one you're with") provided musical contrast, as did the drug culture's hallucinatory images and fantastical metaphors ("Lucy in the sky with diamonds.") Just like the 50s, this era is often played as a cliché rather than the intensely emotional time it truly was.

TODAY

Because the world was growing ever smaller as communication grew, after the Disco rage of the 70's passed, new musical styles rapidly emerged and old musical styles began overlapping. The most profound change for the performer was the advent of the music video. No longer could a popular singer merely sing, but beginning in the 80's, he or she was also expected to act (to a degree) and dance, or at least move (thanks in part to the wireless microphone technology). The intimacy of the soloist gave way to an emphasis on production value and visual spectacle.

"When people go to concerts, they say I'm going to see...not, I'm going to hear." **Branford Marsalis**

Styles began merging in the 80's with styles like country becoming more pop and vice versa, and today there is more of a selection of artists and styles than ever before thanks to the Internet and the iPod. Even musical theatre has adapted to a wide variety of blended styles with such musicals as *Starlight Express, The Best Little Whorehouse in Texas, Rent,* and *In the Heights.*

Nowadays, due to our visual world, the performer must be versatile to survive. Today, not only must you act and dance, you may even be asked to hang from aerial silks as you belt out a song (something the singer, *Pink,* does beautifully, by the way.) You also have to look good. Sex sells and, although there are still songs where "boy meets girl, boy marries girl", they take a backseat to the overt sexual energy of the times. Singers today must have a full command of the range and audiences expect a "belt" sound. Unfortunately, singers often attempt this without the proper training, leading to nodes and lots of cancelled concert dates.

Regardless of the venue, period, or style, the basic principles of singing and acting apply, but few singers can embrace all of the styles since there is so much contrast between opera, musical theatre, jazz, pop, rock, metal, and rap. Even if they could, few would meet the physical expectations the industry requires for each style. (Remember, today the audience listens with their eyes.) However, the more extensive and versatile your training, the more employable you will be.

TYPE

Various styles of music call for various "types", whether it's a vocal type or a physical type. The physical type for a female hip-hop star will be different than that of an opera singer, and certainly so will the voice. Good vocal technique will make you more versatile in regard to type, but there are still going to be limits when it comes to sound and physique. Accepting that you may be better suited for a lyric tenor Broadway role than screaming in a metal belt will not only focus your preparation, but it may preserve your voice. If you are dramatically overweight, you may have to accept the fact that you won't get certain roles or performance opportunities. Not everyone is a Prince Charming or Cinderella, but, hey, they can both be pretty shallow roles. Whether it's your type or your age, accept the facts of life. If you haven't made it in a boy band by age 16, it's probably not going to happen. Conversely, you may have to wait a decade to be cast in certain character roles. Colleges may cast a 22-year-old as a mature magistrate, but professional theatres will not. Don't worry. Sometimes opportunities we miss in our youth are a blessing in disguise, and sometimes waiting for the right roles gives you a longer career after 30. (He who laughs last, often laughs best.)

APPLYING ACTING TO SINGING

Although the preceding overview of style may give you a perspective, it will not be enough to give you an authentic performance. You can't simply read an overview and throw on a costume or wig and expect to understand "style." Instead, you must dig deeper in order to understand the energy, the drive, the WANT, the OBSTACLE, and the IMAGERY that affected the people who lived in a particular time and place.

There are two important questions to ask when you are considering acting and singing in a particular style.

1. Does the action take place in the era the musical work was conceived in? For example, *State Fair* was conceived in *and* set in the 1940's, and *Hair* was conceived in *and* set in the 1960's.

2. Are you performing a work that was conceived in a different era than the one it takes place in? For example, *My Fair Lady* was conceived in the 1950s but takes place in the 19th Century, and *Thoroughly Modern Millie* was conceived in the 1960's but is set in the 1920's.

This later situation will require various compromises since the performer must honor both eras. Although the music may reflect the style it was conceived in, it's probably more important, as an actor, to honor the era it is set in. There's no way to clear this hurdle if you don't understand the characteristics of both.

COSTUMES AND ATTIRE

A flirtation at the turn of the 20th Century, expressed with a coy smile and quick flash of the ankle, is far different than the nudity and the overt sexuality expressed in the musical, *Hair.* How we, as a culture, retain and release energy, sexual or otherwise, is often reflected in what we wear. One period's emphasis on modesty may "suggest" where another's flair and bravado may "announce." A corset or military uniform will affect your posture (and your breathing.). Platform shoes of the 1970's can limit your stride, but so can the bound feet of the ancient Chinese. The costume and costume accessories will affect the dramatic action whether it's the fringe on Velma's dress in *Chicago,* the curlers in Miss Hannigan's hair in *Annie,* or the cowboy hat on Curley's head in *Oklahoma.*

THE EMOTIONAL LANGUAGE OF COLOR AND DICTION

The Italians developed bel canto singing in the 19th Century, a form of "beautiful singing" that is suited to their language of open vowels and crisp, clear consonants. The Germans, whose language is darker and more guttural is suited for the Singspiel, a popular form of German-language opera in which singing alternates with spoken dialogue. The French influenced the Impressionist period with their sensual nasality, while American music, as you've learned, is often steeped in the diphthongs and lingering consonants that characterize the language. Since musical theatre is an American art form, there is more emphasis on the Americanized spoken word than you will find in the bel canto pronunciations in Italian opera. Americans place more emphasis on understanding the words and imbuing them with spoken inflection, whereas Italian opera calls for clarity in the diction, with the words taking a backseat to the sonority of the sound.

> *"If you're dealing with a musical in which you're trying to tell a story, it's got to sound like speech. At the same time, it's got to be a song."*   **Stephen Sondheim**

The color of the language profoundly affects the emotional expression of the work. For example, an American gospel number will lose something in translation if it's sung in French, just as Wagner's operas will lack dramatic intensity if they're sung in English rather than German. This is why it's usually best to perform a work in its original language. If you don't have that luxury, you will need to find an authentic translation of the work in order to honor the text. For example, in Italian, the word "vieni" means "come." The line, "come to me" will certainly affect an actor's imagery and intent. In order to make good acting choices, the singing actor must understand this.

NOTE: How can opera singers performing in a foreign language honor the moment-to-moment acting choices if they don't understand the moment-to-moment language? Thankfully, with a little research, authentic translations can be found for foreign works on the Internet. In fact, "Google Translator" although often unreliable for phrases, comes in handy if you want to quickly look up a word.

Even the subtle acting of a 17th or 18th century art song or aria sung in recital requires an understanding of the language for presentation purposes. The one-size-fits-all posture and attitude of the classically-trained singer must be questioned when it comes to the text and musical accompaniment. Paisiello's "Nel cor piu non mi sento" is a flirtatious musical romp ("He teases me, he pinches me, he squeezes me, he wrenches me"). This is in contrast to the dark text and music of Monteverdi's "Lasciatemi morire" ("Let me die, and what you would think could comfort me in such a harsh fate.") Delivering these two arias without any variation in the physical presentation simply doesn't make sense.

PROPER DICTION VS. EFFECTIVE DICTION

There is a difference between proper diction and effective diction. Certainly, the words are important, so they must be clearly understood, but there is also an emotional expression in diction and that is influenced by style. As you've learned, some styles need crisp clear consonants with open vowels, but the more contemporary styles of American music require relaxed "t's" and throaty "r's" to be honest and effective. The over-articulated "t" would sound ridiculous in a pop song with the lyrics, "right on" or "better and better." "Bedder" may not be proper diction, but it's far more effective for the style. Over-articulation is a little like asking a tap dancer to perform in the style of a ballet dancer on pointe. It simply doesn't suit the style.

For the acting singer, there are other considerations when it comes to diction and color, such as region (your dialect), age (and maturity), social standing (Cockney as opposed to the Queen's English), and personality traits (obnoxious or shy). These elements should not only be considered in the speaking voice, but should be applied to the singing as well. "To what degree" depends on the style and intent. This is best illustrated in *My Fair Lady*. Eliza's speaking voice and singing voice must live in a parallel universe throughout the musical. Early on, she must adapt her Cockney speaking voice to her singing voice when she sings, "Wouldn't It be

Loverly." Later, both her singing and speaking voice must become more refined as she learns the proper way to speak English.

> **NOTE: Keep in mind that dialect is not just about pronunciation. It also has to do with color (the nasality of the French or the lifted palate of the Russian) and body language (the Italian's expressive hands as opposed to the reserved gestures of the Japanese). Also, you must be sure to match the singing voice with the speaking voice of your character when you adopt a dialect. Otherwise, there is an emotional disconnect for both you and your audience.**

> *"The fundamental things apply as time goes by."*
> *Herman Hupfeld*

DON'T FORGET THE BASICS

Whether you are playing a middle-aged, outgoing Russian Jew (Tevye in *Fiddler on the Roof*), a shy, young French orphan (Lily in *Carnival*), or a wise Southern prostitute (Miss Mona in *The Best Little Whorehouse in Texas*), you must still go back to the basics of IMAGERY, FEELING, and FORM to be an effective actor. It will prevent the clichés and arch types that leave the character with no soul or dimension.

EXERCISES

1. *Select a song (preferably not from a musical) that was written after 1900 and before 1980. Find pictures on the Internet or in books that reflect the times it was conceived in. Establish a WHOM and your relationship with the WHOM. Imagine both of you in a setting and dressed in*

204

attire from the period. Create a set of original circumstances and then determine a BACKSTORY, a WANT, an OBJECTIVE, and various OBSTACLES.

Practice singing the song with these parameters, but don't be afraid to try it a variety of ways.

Try out other songs from other decades. Simply allow yourself to time travel and play make-believe.

2. *Listen to recordings from various styles and eras of the past century. Note the variations in diction, vocal color, rhythm, key, phrasing, and orchestrations. Does the diction and vocal color represent the Italian classics, or does it reflect a more relaxed 20th Century American approach? Is the vocal color breathy or focused? Is it sung in head voice or chest voice...or a mix? Is the rhythm syncopated, driving, or laid back? Is the phrasing on the beat or behind it? Are there strings, saxophones, or electronic instruments in the accompaniment?*

   This analysis is important. If you can't recognize the differences while you listen, you won't be able to perform them when you sing.

3. *Decide on an era and immerse yourself in it. Watch reputable films with authentic historical production value of the time or actually watch films made in the era. Read novels, poetry, and journals, and listen to music of the day. Try out some of the popular dance moves of the time, and then let your imagination go. Imagine yourself preparing and/or eating dinner in this period. Imagine your daily chores or those of your servants. Imagine getting dressed in the morning and getting ready for bed at night. How do you and/or your spouse get to work? How do you relate to your peers, your elders, or your lovers? How do you share*

mail? The world news? Gossip? Walk through your period home in your mind, whether it's a Park Avenue suite, an inner city flat, or a log cabin. "Vicariously" (a word every actor should know) enjoy the period.

4. *If possible, visit the costume shop or props room at a local college or high school, and/or spend some time in a vintage clothing store or antique shop. Imagine wearing and/or using the items you encounter. In other words, project yourself into a story that would make use of these items.*

5. *Using a text you have memorized (The Pledge of Allegiance or a simple monologue), repeat it with varied diction and color. You might even try out a dialect or character voice. Just remember to keep it honest, and make sure your IMAGERY and your gestures are connected. After you've spoken the text, sing it with a made-up melody. Try and keep your singing voice and speaking voice aligned.*

6. *After you've observed and imitated a variety of accents and dialects, take a risk (if you are feeling particularly brave). Go to a part of town where no one knows you (or better yet a different state). Pretend to be someone you're not. You don't have to lie to do this, but you can certainly convey a different personality while you pay for your coffee or cash a check at the bank. It's even more fun if you enlist a friend to go along with the charade. It will only be a problem if you run into your mom's best friend or actually encounter another "Swedish hostel tourist."*

7. *Observe and imitate anyone and everyone—family members, both young and old, friends and acquaintances, film and television characters, teachers and colleagues. Make it a point to notice details you might have otherwise ignored. Does your great-aunt's slow shuffled walk make*

you late whenever she's with you? Does her whiny voice irritate you when she's in the car with you? Does the little neighbor boy make you laugh when he talks with a lisp? Is your best friend's loud and overbearing attitude driving you crazy? Why does your grandfather have to talk so loudly? Would it be impossible for your mother to talk if she couldn't use her hands? Although you are exploring your present universe, you will increase your powers of observation and that will ultimately help you recreate a more foreign character.

When you imitate the traits you observe, it doesn't have to be in a literal way. Instead, you can borrow certain traits and add them to your own personality.

*At this point you've observed these people from **your** vantage point. Now look at these traits from **their** vantage point by asking yourself "why?" Does your aunt shuffle due to a bad hip? Does she whine because she gets more attention that way? Is the little neighbor boy adjusting to his lack of front teeth due to a fall from his bike? Is your best friend overcompensating for her insecurities? Is your grandfather hard of hearing? Is your mother's use of her hands cultural or is it just part of her high-energy personality?*

THE WHOLE POINT...

When you understand and imitate those around you, you will learn how to understand and imitate those who are more foreign to you. When you understand "why" people act a certain way, you become more empathetic and begin to feel their joys and sorrows. Ultimately, this will help you avoid assumptions and eliminate prejudices. And who knows? Maybe that's the secret to a better world.

> *"I love acting. It is so much more real than life."*
> *Oscar Wilde*

People often ask theatre artists what it's like to live in a fake world, but performing artists realize early on that the aesthetic process that connects them to the human condition and the technique that allows them to explore and share feelings that shape lives *IS* the real world. It's certainly more real than the "Hello. How are you?" from the local convenience store clerk or the formal conversation at a job interview. And yet, there are those moments in our "real" lives that transform reality—those moments that can only be truly expressed with a soaring melodic underscore or poetic metaphor. So who's to say what's real and what's not? Who's to say that life and art isn't the same thing? William Shakespeare understood this when he wrote:

> *All the world's a stage*
> *And all the men and women merely players*
> *They have their exits and their entrances*
> *And one man in his time plays many parts*

The point of *"What Do I Do with My Hands?"* isn't to provide you with all the answers. It is designed to provide tools for a process that will teach you how to ask and answer your own questions. Hopefully, now that you've read the text and committed to the exercises, you will begin to develop your own technique, but even that should be challenged. You should study other approaches as you expand your rehearsal and performance opportunities. Eventually, you will learn to embrace what works and discard what doesn't.

The performing arts can be frustrating, but the rewards are great if you have the courage to put yourself out there and take some risks. You won't know your limits until you've tested them, and then once you think you've reached your limits, you should challenge them. The most important thing is to never lose the awe and wonder that brought you to the performing arts in the first place.

> *"If we, citizens, do not support our artists, then we sacrifice our imagination on the altar of crude reality and we end up believing in nothing and having worthless dreams."* **Yann Martel, Life of Pi**

Bibliography

Adler, Stella; Kissel, Howard. *Stella Adler on the Art and Technique of Acting.* New York: Applause Theatre and Cinema Books. 2000

Barton, Robert. *Style for Actors: A Handbook for Moving Beyond Realism.* New York: Routledge.2010

Csikszentmihalyi, Mihaly. *Creativity: Flow and the Psychology of Discovery and Invention.* New York: HarperCollins Publishers. 1996

Hagen, Uta. *Respect for Acting.* New York: MacMillan Publishing Co. 1973

Langer, Susanne K. *Philosophy in a New Key: A Study in the Symbolism of Reason, Rite, and Art.* New York: The New American Library. 1951

Lerner, Alan J. *The Street Where I Live.* New York: W. W. Norton, 1978.

Meisner, Sanford; Longwell, Dennis. *Sanford Meisner on Acting.* New York: Random House Inc. 1987

Owen, Mack. *The Actor's Scenebook.* New York: Harper Collins College Publishers. 1993

Pink, Daniel H. *A Whole New Mind: Why Right-Brainers Will Rule the World.* New York: The Penguin Group. 2006

Shurtleff, Michael. *Audition: Everything an Actor Needs to Know to Get the Part.* New York: Walker Publishing Co. 1978

Silver, Fred. *Auditioning for the Musical Theatre.* New York: Newmarket Press. 1985.

Referenced Works

(See additional repertoire lists after Chapters 1, 2, 3, 5, and 13)

ALL SHOOK UP   E. Presley

ANNIE   C. Strouse/M. Charnin

BIG RIVER   R. Miller

"Bohemian Rhapsody"   Queen

CAMELOT   A.J. Lerner/F. Loewe

CAN CAN   C. Porter
   "I Love Paris"

CARNIVAL   B. Merrill

CAROUSEL   R. Rodgers/O. Hammerstein
   "Soliloquy"

CINDERELLA   R. Rodgers/O. Hammerstein
   "In My Own Little Corner"

COMPANY   S. Sondheim
   "Getting Married Today"

DREAMGIRLS   H. Krieger
   "And I am Telling You, I'm Not Going

EVENING PRIMROSE   S. Sondheim
   "I Remember"

EVITA   A.L Webber/T. Rice

FIDDLER ON THE ROOF   J. Bock/S. Harnick
   "Far From the Home I Love"

FLORA, THE RED MENACE   J. Kander/F. Ebb
   "It's a Quiet Thing"

GIGI   A. J. Lerner/F. Loewe
   "Yes, I Remember It Well "

GREASE   J. Jacobs, W. Casey

HAIR   J. Rado/G. MacDermot

HAIRSPRAY   M. Shaiman/S. Wittman
        "You Can't Stop the Beat"

"Hey, Good Lookin"   H. Williams

HOW TO SUCCEED IN BUSINESS   F. Loesser

"I'll be Seeing You"   `   S. Fain/I. Kahal

IN THE HEIGHTS   Lin-Manuel Miranda

INTO THE WOODS   S. Sondheim

"It Was a Very Good Year"   E. Drake

JESUS CHRIST SUPERSTAR   A.L. Webber/T. Rice
        "Gethsemane"

KISS ME KATE   C. Porter
        "I Hate Men"

LES MISERABLES   C.M. Schonberg/A. Boublil
      "Bring Him Home" – "Castle on a Cloud"
      "Do You Heart the People Sing" – "I Dreamed a Dream"

"Love the One You're With"   S. Stills

"Lucy in the Sky With Diamonds"   J. Lennon, P. McCartney

MAN OF LA MANCHA   M. Leigh/J. Darion
        "I Really Like Him"

MY FAIR LADY   A. J. Lerner/F. Loewe
      "I Could Have Danced All Night"-"Just You Wait, Henry Higgins"
      "Wouldn't It Be Loverly?"

OKLAHOMA   R. Rodgers/O. Hammerstein
        "Oh, What a Beautiful Morning"

OLIVER   L. Bart

PETER PAN   M. Charlap/C. Leigh
        "I'm Flying"

PIRATES OF PENZANCE	W.S. Gilbert/A. Sullivan
RENT	J. Larson
SEUSSICAL	S. Flaherty
SHOWBOAT	J. Kern/O. Hammerstein
"Smile"	C. Chaplin/J. Turner/ G. Parsons
SOUTH PACIFIC "I'm in Love with a Wonderful Guy"	R. Rodgers/O. Hammerstein
STARLIGHT EXPRESS	A. L. Webber/R. Stilgoe
STATE FAIR	R. Rodgers/O. Hammerstein
"Stop in the Name of Love"	Holland-Dozier-Holland
SUNDAY IN THE PARK WITH GEORGE "Putting it Together"	S. Sondheim
THE BEST LITTLE WHOREHOUSE IN TEXAS	C. Hall
THE LAST FIVE YEARS	J.R. Brown
THE SOUND OF MUSIC "Climb Every Mountain"- "Favorite Things"	R. Rodgers/O. Hammerstein
"The Way We Were"	A. Bergman/M. Bergman
THE WIZ	C. Smalls
THOROUGHLY MODERN MILLIE "Not For the Life of Me"	J. Tesori/D. Scanlan
WEST SIDE STORY "Tonight"	L. Bernstein/S. Sondheim
WICKED "Defying Gravity"	S. Schwartz

For additional updates to the repertoire list, visit:
www.RhondaCarlsonStudio.com

INDEX

About Rhonda Carlson

Rhonda Carlson serves as an international workshop clinician, specializing in acting for the singer. Besides a long performance career in music and theatre, as well as a directing resume of over 200 productions, Rhonda has nearly 40 years of performing arts teaching experience. She has taught music and/or theatre at such schools as The Boston Conservatory, Boston University and The University of Southern Maine, and her students have performed on Broadway, in national tours, on television, in film, and have been accepted into some of the most prestigious performing arts programs in the world. As a composer, she has composed scores for film, and as a composer/playwright, her musical, *Dear Emma*, has received critical acclaim from The LA Times, as well as numerous other sources. In 2009, her play, *Fly Over Land*, won the 2009 Larry Corse International Playwriting Competition. Rhonda resides in Las Vegas with her husband, Kevan, and her daughters, Laura and Kayla.

Ordering and Contact Information

For individual copies of this book:

Check with your local bookstore or with your favorite online book seller. Also available at:

www.Amazon.com

Case-lot orders for resale, educational and non-profit purposes:

www.PersonalDynamicsPublishing.com

For additional products, services and seminars from Rhonda Carlson, please contact:

www.RhondaCarlsonStudio.com

55456606R00124

Made in the USA
Middletown, DE
10 December 2017